500   Check Dean

SO-AIS-113

Review Notes and Study Guide

to

The Canterbury Tales

of

CHAUCER

by JOSEPH GRENNEN, Ph.D.
Department of English,
Fordham University

EDITORIAL BOARD OF CONSULTANTS

STANLEY COOPERMAN, PH.D.
Department of English
Hofstra University

CHARLES LEAVITT, PH.D.
Department of English
Montclair State College

UNICIO J. VIOLI, PH.D.
Department of English
Fairleigh Dickinson University

Distributed by:
MONARCH PRESS, INC.
387 Park Avenue South
New York 16, N. Y.

© 1963 by Thor Publications, Inc., New York, N. Y.
© 1964 by Thor Publications, Inc., New York
All rights reserved. No part of this book may be
reproduced without the written permission of the
publisher.

TABLE OF CONTENTS

PREFACE

yone who presumes to add another book to the growing list of outlines,
mmentaries, modernizations—even children's versions—of Chaucer's
try must begin with an apology. Modernizations (and there are some
d ones) tend sometimes to be even more difficult than Chaucer's Middle
glish text; the existing outlines and commentaries are frequently filled
h a riot of information about scholarly problems, or else are so sketchy,
t they bear only a remote resemblance to the poems themselves. I am
course not referring to the works of scholarship and literary criticism
ch have, in the last two decades, enlightened us about Chaucer's meaning
haps more than all the literary discussion of the five centuries past.
these are often beyond reach—and beyond the needs—of the audience
book is designed to serve. It may well be that for any number of
sons pupils in secondary schools should not be asked to come to grips
the subtleties of Chaucer. And the arguments could be put almost as
ngly for college undergraduates. But there are riches in Chaucer's
try—wisdom, humor, pathos, even invective and satire—which the
escent mind can respond to. And despite the difficulties, Chaucer is
g taught in our high schools and junior colleges.

overwhelming problem facing anyone who tries to translate or re-tell
ucer's stories, is that he was himself a re-teller of other men's
ies. The modern version, therefore, may well turn out to be much
er to Chaucer's source than to Chaucer's own poetry. It is in the
guage itself—in the untranslatable suggestiveness—that much of
ucer's meaning lies. Somehow, the modern version must give a hint
what Chaucer was up to—what he saw in the original source, and what
of shaping art he used in adapting it. With all this in view, and
embering the relatively unformed (and uninformed) minds encountering
strangeness of Chaucer's verse for the first time, I have adopted
e principles as a guide in the summation and commentaries which
e up the book:

To re-tell the story in outline form, in easily understandable
guage, yet, as far as possible, with a Chaucerian inflection.

To make Chaucer's characters and situations (within reason, and
ding really ludicrous comparisons) comprehensible in modern terms.

To avoid controversial opinions, untried theories, and advanced
ical views (especially to avoid murky critical terminology); at the
e time to ignore textual problems, and questions of the dating and
ering of tales, in favor of purely literary considerations and more
le summaries.

To omit nothing truly Chaucerian merely on the ground that it may
nd the taste of some readers, yet to avoid possibly inflammatory
ils and to omit those words (even though Chaucer used them) which
generally considered obscene.

5.   Finally, to avoid critical generalities, and to concentrate on pa
ticulars.   I find, for instance, that it is of little use to the student to
told that Chaucer was a master of the dramatic method, but that it
genuinely helpful for him to know that the apparently aimless, rand
course of events in the Knight's Tale is intimately related to the m:
theme of the poem, which is concerned with the proper human attitude
strike in the face of the imponderable heavenly logic behind the visi
surface of things.

The "Comments," interspersed in the text, are by no means exhausti
They are meant to clear up crucial points of interpretation, or to sugg
critical attitudes that may be useful at other points in the narrative
well. I have not observed strict proportions in the allotment of space;
General Prologue, and some of the more important tales, like the Nu
Priest's Tale, are given disproportionately lengthy treatment. The bc
does not pretend to be a work of criticism or of scholarship, though it
hoped that it will be found to be based on sound scholarship and defensi
critical opinions. If it is an aid to the youthful reader, if it helps him
find his way through Chaucer—and back to Chaucer—it will have ser
its purpose.

GENERAL INTRODUCTION

SOCIAL BACKGROUND: Geoffrey Chaucer, who was born aro
1340 and died in 1400, lived through a social and religious storm wh
has hardly been equalled in the history of the English nation. The Fo
teenth Century of romantic story—a quaint society of jolly mille
rollicking friars, and amiable outlaws, of distant, fragile ladies :
well-bred knights—is a far cry from the actual facts. And it is iro
that the Canterbury Tales themselves should have endured in the popu
imagination as a reflection of that kind of world. England, in Chauce
day, a country of perhaps four million people, was devastated by
Black Plague in 1349-50. Its population was practically cut in half.
ensuing shortage of farm labor sharpened an already existing cl:
conflict, a conflict which led finally to the terrible Peasants' Revol
1381. A number of unpopular noblemen were lynched in the uprising,
despite Richard II's promise of amnesty, severe reprisals were ta
against the commoners who had played any part in the rebellion. Ville
(serfs bound to the soil), escaping from their lords' estates, took ref
in the towns or joined lawless bands in the forests, which were s
wild, and the subject of superstitious beliefs. Even a masterless m
trained in the use of the English long bow, might find service with
army destined for France, which was attacked and plundered consta
throughout the Hundred Years War (1337-1453). Feudalism, as an econo
system, and chivalry, as a military system, were both in a process
decay. Life, for most people, was hard, violent, and competitive.

ELIGIOUS BACKGROUND: The religious picture was no rosier. The urch, in its upper ranks, was beset by political maneuvering among the shops, and frequent resentment against Roman control; in its lower nks it suffered from the existence of an extraordinary number of rrupt officials, ignorant priests, and wayward parishioners. And ere was an unremitting struggle for dominance between ecclesiastical urts and the King's courts. John Wyclif, the "Morning Star of the formation," was a contemporary of Chaucer's. From an initial attack the worldliness and ignorance of the lower clergy, he moved to a retical denial of such basic church doctrines as the transubstantiation the Eucharist. The church in England, however, did survive the rruption and incompetence of its members, and the attacks from thout. Chaucer himself, by nature a conservative man, could satirize the corruption he observed without putting himself outside the church, and remained a loyal Catholic.

TELLECTUAL BACKGROUND: There is always a tendency to think past periods of civilization as foolish and benighted. Yet the average human intelligence, and the number of geniuses, probably does not vary ach from century to century. The Fourteenth Century was, in fact, a ne of active intellectual probing, and it had its great thinkers— ilosophers like William of Ockham, scientists such as Nicolas Oresme, d medical theorists like John Arderne. The question of free will vs. terminism, the physical nature of sound and light, and the development a surgical technique for the treatment of fistula, for instance, were all bjects of scholarly investigation. Of course, these were not the days of assive popular education, nor was there really any wide circulation of oks. Chaucer, however, was an extremely well-read man for his nes, and his poetry in places has a very bookish quality to it. To judge om the kinds of allusion he makes, he expected his audience to have me direct acquaintance with books both of a scholarly and a popular rt. Romantic stories of love, saints' lives and legends, sermon col- ctions, encyclopedias, and philosophical and theological treatises are a w of the types of literature he refers to. Chaucer seems to have been ry fortunate, indeed, in having a courtly audience which was cultured, phisticated, sensitive, and socially aware.

HAUCER'S LIFE: As might be expected, very little is known of aucer's life. He was born probably around the year 1340. He came om a family of vintners (wine merchants). Somehow he became attached a page to a branch of the royal family, and there is some evidence that may have been in the service of King Edward III himself. While still very young man, he saw military service abroad, and was several times aployed as a royal emissary to the European continent. In the 1370's aucer made a trip to Italy, where he probably picked up a fair knowledge the Italian language, and became acquainted with the works of the great lian authors, notably Dante and Boccaccio. In 1374 he was given a civil rvice position as Controller of Customs, and from that point on held a riety of offices, continuing to act from time to time as a royal repre- ntative. That he was a respected and trustworthy public servant is oved by the record of annuities and pensions he received, and by the ct that toward the end of his life he was given the important post of erk of the King's Works. Upon his death in 1400 he was buried in estminster Abbey. A study of even these sketchy facts leads to the lowing conclusions, important for an understanding of Chaucer's poetry:

1.   Chaucer was himself a shrewd, sophisticated person, toughened a life of hard and complex experiences.

2.   He was a man learned in the French, Italian, and Latin literatures.

3.   Literature was an avocation (spare-time occupation) for him, rath than a full-time job. It was not a money-making proposition.

LITERARY CAREER: It is customary to divide Chaucer's litera career into three parts:

1.   Period of French influence: Chaucer's earliest poetry is sometim a rather pretty and artificial affair. He was experimenting with rhyth and structure, and tended to use conventional and even hackneyed (ove worked) images and ideas. But his originality can be detected even in h earliest work.   The Book of the Duchess is perhaps the most importa poem of this period.   It is first of all a dream-vision, that is, a poem which the author pretends that he has fallen asleep, and that the substan of the poem has come to him in a dream. Secondly, it is an elegy—a poe lamenting the death of a beloved person. Thirdly, it is a consolation, th is, a work which tries to comfort someone's grief by explaining the natu of the forces which have caused it. The Book of the Duchess laments t death of Blanche, Duchess of Lancaster, and is an attempted consolati of her husband (Chaucer's patron), John of Gaunt, Duke of Lancaste Chaucer pretends that in his dream he has become involved in a hunt, a has been led to the figure of a man in black, who is lost in grief. In t course of the dream, Chaucer prods this man into revealing the reaso for his sorrow, and thus helps to cure him of it.

2.   Period of Italian influence: Chaucer certainly knew the works of t great poet, Dante, but he seems to have made more use of the poems Boccaccio.   The greatest of Chaucer's completed poems, Troilus a Criseyde, is based upon the Filostrato of Boccaccio. This poem, in fi books, relates the tragedy of a young Trojan hero, Troilus, who spen the better part of three books pining away for the love of Criseyd Criseyde finally grants him her love, but shortly after is made to jo her father (a traitor) in the Greek camp, and falls in love with Diomed thus proving unfaithful to Troilus. The poem is actually a magnifice and complex treatment of the roles played by human love, Divine Lov free will, and chance (or fortune) in the affairs of men.

3.   Period of so-called "realism:" This is the period of the Canterbu Tales. Chaucer seems, in later life, to have grown away from pure literary models, and to have concentrated more upon the teeming soci life around him.   Students of Chaucer have been so impressed by t lifelike quality of the Canterbury pilgrims, that they have been led search old records for the real life models on which they believe Chauc to have based them. It is not impossible that the poet had real perso in mind for some of the pilgrims, but there is a limit to how far th search can be useful in helping modern readers to appreciate the poe In many subtle ways the Canterbury Tales is still the product of litera models, and of wide reading as well as of actual experience in the world.

THE CANTERBURY TALES: Summary: Chaucer stops off at t Tabard Inn on his way to Canterbury to visit the shrine of Saint Thom

à Becket. He falls in with twenty-nine other pilgrims, and in the famous General Prologue to the Canterbury Tales, describes them for us in great detail. All walks of life, from the lofty Knight to the lowly Plowman, are represented there. Under the guidance of the innkeeper, Harry Bailly, the pilgrims are each to tell two tales on the way to Canterbury and two on the way back. The Knight's Tale is first (a long romance), followed by the Miller's Tale (a short, realistic story). The Miller provokes the Reeve, who tells a nasty story at the expense of millers. And so it goes, one story leading to another. At least that was the general plan. But the poem is fragmentary; Chaucer never lived to complete it or to make a final arrangement of even the parts which he did complete. There are dramatic outbursts, as, for example, when the Host offers a vile insult to the Pardoner and they almost come to blows. But the Knight steps in and acts the part of peacemaker. Some tales are grouped around a single theme, marriage, for instance, and explore different aspects of that theme. The Nun's Priest's Tale makes fun of the idea of tragedy, which the Monk has advanced so solemnly in his tale. The Parson's Tale, which is the last, is a long sermon which Chaucer apparently intended to be a kind of unifying element, bringing all themes to rest in a Christian framework. At the very end is a Retraction, in which Chaucer takes back all the sinful things he wrote and asks forgiveness and rest for his soul.

The Canterbury Tales can be looked at from any one of several points of view:

1. As an anthology (or cross-section) of medieval literary types: Almost every type of medieval literature is represented here. The Knight's Tale is a romance, the Miller's Tale a fabliau, the Second Nun's Tale a saint's legend, the Prioresses Tale a "miracle of the virgin." There are sermons, beast fables, contemporary anecdotes, and allegories; in short, it is a virtual storehouse of the kinds of literature to be found in Chaucer's day.

2. As the story of a pilgrimage: The pilgrims are, after all, on their way to Canterbury. This notion of religious veneration colors all the tales, and all the incidents which arise on the way. The themes and ideas expressed by the pilgrims (whether they are offered seriously or ironically) have to be measured against the kind of religious ideal which the shrine of the great martyr stands for. For example, it is impossible to read the Franklin's Tale, which deals with human integrity, without judging the characters in the light of the saintly integrity which Thomas himself displayed in his martyrdom.

3. As a representative view of fourteenth-century English society: For one thing, the gallery of portraits in the General Prologue covers the whole range of fourteenth-century occupations and professions. We have a knight, a lawyer, a doctor, a merchant, a parson, and so forth. It also covers an entire range of people considered in terms of folly and wisdom. The Parson is virtue pure and simple; the Pardoner is a thoroughly vicious scoundrel; and there are all sorts of gradations in between. The Manciple is wise (though unscrupulous), while the Clerk seems just a bit of a ninny; again, we can find shadings between. The tales themselves are not just idle entertainment but deal with important social and domestic issues. Who should wear the pants in the family? (Wife of Bath's Tale) How should guardians raise the children of their

lords? (Physician's Tale) Is there any truth in the science of alchemy? (Canon's Yeoman's Tale) As a practical man of affairs Chaucer undoubtedly saw some of his tales as offering guides to proper social conduct.

4. As a framed story: The variety and the diversity in the characters and their tales is given an over-all unity, basically, by the device of the framed story. That is, Chaucer invented the scheme of a pilgrimage to make realistic and effective the story-telling and the interplay of character. We do not know what gave him the idea, or, indeed, if he really needed any model for it. The notion of a pilgrimage as a basis for a story collection is not so very unusual, after all. He may have been influenced by earlier story collections like the Decameron of Boccaccio, or Ovid's Metamorphoses (which he knew well), and he may even have been influenced simply by seeing pilgrimages passing his house on their way to Canterbury. In any case, the frame gives the poem at least a kind of artificial unity. It consists of the General Prologue, occasional head-links and end-links (short sections relating things that happened on the way), prologues to individual tales, and a few interruptions by a pilgrim in the middle of someone else's tale (the Pardoner interrupts the Wife of Bath, for instance).

Connected with the idea of the frame, is the poet's conception of the narrator's personality. Of course, it is narrated by Geoffrey Chaucer. But, as is frequently the case in literature (compare it with Gulliver's Travels, for example), the personality Chaucer gives his narrator is a far cry from the actual personality of Chaucer himself. In his fictional character he allows himself to be taken in by the most outrageous examples of vice and hypocrisy. He pretends to have no literary judgment at all (he gives himself the absolutely worst tale to tell—Sir Thopas), and he ridicules his own appearance. In the final analysis, whatever unity the poem does possess is a result of the framing device, the character of the narrator, and the thematic connections between tales, all working together in a fairly harmonious fashion.

THE GENERAL PROLOGUE

INTRODUCTION: Chaucer begins his poem with a leisurely and flowery description of the English countryside in the Springtime. All the animals and especially the birds are prodded by instinct into participation in the processes of Nature. Nightingales, by nature, sing all the night through—and people find themselves stirred to go off on pilgrimages. In England, the chief pilgrimage is to the shrine of Thomas a Becket, the martyr of Canterbury. Chaucer happens to be just such a pilgrim and he has stopped off for the night at the Tabard Inn, located in Southwerk, a suburb of London. As he takes his rest there, a group of twenty-nine people, of all walks of life, who had banded together by chance, enter the

Inn to put up for the night before beginning their pilgrimage to Canterbury. Chaucer, being a naturally friendly fellow, joins their party and manages, in conversation, to find out a great deal of information about each of them. He describes them for us, one by one.

THE KNIGHT: The Knight is the equivalent of a modern field-grade officer, perhaps a lieutenant-colonel. He is a dedicated soldier, a lover of "trouthe and honour, fredom and curteisie" (in modern terms, "integrity and honor, generosity and gentility"). He has, so to speak, a chestful of campaign ribbons. He has gone to the far corners of Christendom in defense of his God and King. Not only has he been involved in fifteen battles to the death, but he has been in a single combat (in tournaments) three separate times. For all his accomplishments he is a humble and meek man—"a verray, parfit, gentil knyght."

> **COMMENT:**   The Knight is easily the most socially prominent person· on the pilgrimage. The fact that Chaucer begins by describing him shows the poet's awareness of social status.

THE SQUIRE: The Knight's son, the young squire, is roughly equivalent to an officer candidate. He is strong, handsome, lithe, with curly hair (fashionable, even for men). On military campaigns on the continent the squire had handled himself very well, hoping to win the good graces of his favorite young lady. During peacetime he was lighthearted indeed, singing or fluting all the day. He could ride a horse well, compose songs, dash off a passable letter, and even paint pictures. Doing all things well, he made no exception in the case of love. He loved so hotly, Chaucer says, that he slept no more than a nightingale.

> **COMMENT:**   Chaucer's portrait suggests that the Squire, while he was an admirable youth, fancied himself something of a ladies' man.   This is not a damning accusation, but it alerts us to the fact that Chaucer is not easily taken in by sham. Suggestions of this sort, of course, are never baldly stated. Exaggeration, irony, and subtle innuendo are present in the narrator's words, though he himself rarely seems conscious of the implications of his words.

THE YEOMAN: The Yeoman is nothing less than a master forester. He is dressed all in green, carries a sheaf of peacock-feathered arrows, bright and sharp, and bears a mighty bow. He knows all the arts of woodcraft, and is also prepared for combat, with a sword, buckler, and dagger at his side. Though rough and ready, he is a devout man, as the silver St. Christopher medal on his breast proves.

THE PRIORESS: Here we have a portrait of a very elegant fourteenth-century lady who also happens to be a nun, and a convent official. She is very well educated; she knows how to sing the divine services (though she sings through her nose), and she can speak French (but with a broad English accent).   The Prioress is almost excessively dainty, pleasant, and sensitive. She never dips her fingers in the gravy, Chaucer tells us, and she grabs for her food in a very modest way. But her outstanding trait is her sensitivity. So full of charity and sympathy is she that she weeps at the sight of a mouse in a trap, or of a dog being beaten with a stick. Her clothing is neat, and her features are impressively handsome.

She carries a set of rosary beads, on which there is a gold brooch bearing the motto "Amor vincit omnia."

> **COMMENT:** The motto means "Love conquers all." Of course, for a person in the religious life Divine Love is the most important factor. But there are other kinds of love, and this sly sort of suggestion runs through the entire portrait. The Prioress is a wonderful nun, we assume, but she never ceases to be a woman.

THE NUN-PRIEST GROUP:

At this point Chaucer mentions another Nun (she later narrates the Second Nun's Tale), and three priests with the Prioress. One of these is the teller of the Nun's Priest's Tale. The other two are never mentioned again, and none of them are described here.

THE MONK:

The Monk is a robust individual, who likes riding and hunting. (Chaucer asserts that for his "manliness" he would probably make a good abbot.) He has no use, however, for the time-honored rules of the monastic orders, which required a very prayerful, solitary, and pleasureless existence. This monk thinks he is simply being modern in preferring fine clothes, racing, and other luxuries, to the hard life of St. Augustine or St. Benedict. He has a bald head, a shining face with deep-set eyes, and he rides a brown palfrey.

> **COMMENT:** Chaucer pretends to be taken in by the arguments which clerics like the Monk use to justify their worldly lives. But we can read between the lines and see the vicious satire against churchmen who lead sinful lives and are proud of it.

THE FRIAR:

The Friar is even more vicious than the Monk, and yet Chaucer pretends to be greatly impressed by his good qualities.

> **COMMENT:** Friars were members of preaching orders. They traveled from parish to parish, giving sermons and hearing confessions of sins. Because parish priests were notorious for the hard penances they imposed on the people, the friars became popular by giving easy penances. In time they used their great powers to their own advantage, taking money (and perhaps other pleasures) from the ignorant people they should have been helping.

Chaucer's Friar is typical. He has made a good thing out of his license to hear confessions. He gives an easy penance (when he knows he will be paid off handsomely for it). He carries about a bag full of knives and pins, to get on the good side of the ladies. But strangely for a Friar (even the narrator thinks it is strange) he knows the taverns and the inns better than he knows the leper-houses and the alms-houses. If the ability to pry money out of people is the mark of a successful mendicant (begging friar), then this man, Hubert is his name, is the best beggar in the order, bar none.

THE MERCHANT:

The Merchant is a business man. He is something like the modern director of a big corporation. He is always delivering weighty opinions, and constantly talking business and boasting about all the money he has earned. He wishes the government would do something to protect the English businessman against pirates. The Merchant is shrewd, and he drives a hard bargain when he buys and sells money on the exchange.

But he was quite dignified, and even though he talks in business jargon everyone seems to like him.

THE CLERK:
The Clerk is an Oxford-educated scholar. He has graduated long ago, but he doesn't seem to have done anything practical with his life. He rides a skinny horse, and he is not much fatter himself. His overcoat is worn to the last thread. Even at his advanced age, he has not yet gotten a position either in the Church or in civil government. The reason seems to be that he is a kind of idealist—a scholar, pure and simple. He'd rather spend money on twenty volumes of Aristotle's works than use it to buy wine, women, and song. He lives on what he can borrow from his friends and relatives, and he spends most of that on books. With all his learning, he is something of a pedant (one who parades his knowledge). And his speech is filled with high-sounding words, and bits of moral advice.

THE SERGEANT OF THE LAW:
This man is not only a lawyer but has frequently been called on to serve as a judge in the very highest courts. He is undoubtedly very wise, but the legal terms he is always using make him appear even wiser. Unlike the Clerk, he is very much interested in using his learning to make money. He knew how to make it—and he knew how to spend it. He is constantly bustling around looking busy, though Chaucer gets the impression that he looks busier than he really is. He could quote you case after case, and decision after decision, all the way back to William the Conqueror. He is a regular walking law library.

COMMENT:
Satire against money-grubbing lawyers is an old literary convention. Chaucer is simply repeating ancient accusations, though there were undoubtedly many fourteenth-century lawyers who could fill the bill.

THE FRANKLIN:
A Franklin was a kind of country gentleman. This Franklin seems to be very conscious of his wealth, and at the same time spends it freely on food and drink—for himself and his friends. He was a real connoisseur. Every morning he would begin the day by having a piece of bread dipped in wine. This gave him a rather rosy complexion (and perhaps a rosy outlook on things). Nobody had a better supply of bread, ale, and wine. It literally snowed food and liquor in his house, and all the dainty dishes you could think of. God help the cook if the gravy wasn't just right, or if the table wasn't set properly. In fact, most of the time the table just stood set for meals the whole day through. For all his pleasure-seeking, he seems to have been looked up to by his friends. He had been a knight of the shire, and even a sheriff on one occasion.

THE GUILDSMEN:
Belonging to a guild was like belonging to an organization which was a combination of a labor union and a national association of manufacturers. On Chaucer's pilgrimage there were five Guildsmen: a Haberdasher, a Carpenter, a Weaver, a Dyer, and a Tapestrymaker. They were all members of the same Guild and wore the same distinguishing clothing. They are recent successes (what today we call nouveau riche), and very proud of it. Their knives and purses are decorated with silver, and they are quite smug (as are their wives) about the material advantages they can afford. "It's very nice to be called 'Sir,' and 'Madam,'

and have people open doors for you," they seem to be saying by their glances.

THE COOK:
The Cook accompanies the Gildsmen. He is a master of his trade—something like the head chef at the Waldorf. He can roast, simmer, boil, and fry; he knows how to turn out a variety of main dishes and desserts. "But you know," the narrator says (with tongue in cheek), "I think it's rather a shame that he happens to have a running sore on his shin."

THE SHIPMAN:
The Shipman is of course no common sailor, but a Master of a vessel. He came from Dartmouth, in the west country. The Shipman, though not an ordinary roughneck, was a tough customer. Burned brown from the sun, a dagger hanging around his neck on a lanyard, and fortified with many a healthy swallow of wine, he made an impressive appearance. Whenever there was a sea battle, and boarding parties took to the deck, he didn't stand on ceremony. If he got the upper hand he pitched his enemy overboard without getting conscience-stricken about it. He is a real sea-going man, and a shrewd navigator. He knows the tides, the stars, and the harbors from the Mediterranean to the Baltic.

THE DOCTOR OF PHYSIC:
By modern standards fourteenth-century medicine was pretty primitive. But making allowances for this, the Doctor is a magnificent example of a physician and surgeon. Today, he would be a Chief of a Service at a big metropolitan hospital (a Gillespie rather than a Kildare). He knew his astronomy and his natural magic; and he knew the causes of every disease, whether they came from heat or cold, or moisture or dryness. He knew where they originated, and what "humor" they came from.

> **COMMENT:** Medieval people thought there were four "humors," or fluids which made up the liquid content of the human body. These were blood, phlegm, black bile, and yellow bile. If a person had them in exactly equal proportions, he was a "well-balanced individual, physically and mentally. If the proportions were off, he might act like a "character," (gloomy, or cranky, or excessively optimistic, for instance), or he might be treated as physically ill. Chaucer is not criticizing the Doctor for believing in the ''humors'' theory, though there is a slight suggestion that he is just a little too ready to diagnose a disease before the examination was complete.

The Doctor is a good practitioner, but he is in cahoots with the druggist (an old complaint). They are operating a fee-splitting scheme. And, like the lawyer, the Doctor is a bit too ready to quote his medical authorities— and he knows plenty of them: Aesculapius, Galen, Hippocrates, Rhazes, Avicenna, and a dozen others. About the Bible, however, he knows very little. (This is a frequent complaint against doctors in the Middle Ages. "Where you have three doctors you'll find two atheists," was an oft-quoted statement.) The portrait ends with a jibe at the Doctor's stinginess. Whatever he earned during plague-time (and it must have been a lot) he was very slow to spend; and because gold (in solution) was a medical treatment—a heart stimulant, to be specific—he had a very special love of gold.

THE WIFE OF BATH: The Wife is introduced as if being a wife were a profession, like law or medicine. The humorous thing is, that in this wife's case, that is very close to being true. Dame Alice of Bath, for that is her name and her home town, has had five husbands, and is on the prowl for a sixth.   She is a tremendous woman, with a bold face and a ruddy complexion.   She rules the roost in her own parish, and no other woman would dare to go up to the altar and make an offering before Alice had done so.   Chaucer is willing to swear that her Sunday head-coverings weighed a full ten pounds; and with her red stockings and fine new leather shoes, she cut quite a swath through town.   Moreover, Alice was a dyed-in-the-wool pilgrim, and when Spring came there was no holding her back from Canterbury, Rome, St. James of Compostella, and any number of other shrines.   She is riding an ambler and wearing a hat as broad as a shield, a blanket tied around her hips, and a pair of spurs on her feet. She could tell a good story with the best (or the worst) of the men in the group.

THE TOWN PARSON: In a band of wordly clerics, hypocrites, and other assorted knaves and fools, the Parson stands out like a sore thumb. He really <u>did</u> follow the gospel of Christ. Devout, diligent, and patient, he would rather pay a parishioner's church-tax out of his own pocket than to curse him for it.   This Parson's parish was spread out far and wide, but he never failed to visit the sick—far and near, rich and poor alike. "What can we expect of the common people if their spiritual leaders are frauds," was his feeling on the matter.   And he didn't go running off to London to become a chapel priest, on a fat salary, and leave his own flock in the lurch.   And while he wasn't spiteful, or stand-offish to sinful people, he wasn't soft-headed either.   He knew how to administer a sharp rebuke when it was needed.   Good example—Christ's example—was his ruling principle.

THE PLOWMAN: The Plowman is the Parson's brother. He, too, is no phony. He has pitched many a forkful of dung over the pasture fence.

> **COMMENT:**   By making the Plowman and the Parson brothers, Chaucer is able to suggest that reform of the Church had to be based upon a union of simple, <u>basic</u> people. The Parson provides the spiritual food, and the Plowman supplies the bread and the meat.   The Plowman (and this is emphasized in the great poem, <u>Piers Plowman</u>, by Chaucer's contemporary, William Langland) was the backbone of fourteenth-century society.

The Plowman has all the simple virtues. He loves God and his neighbor; he helps those in need; and he pays his tithes (church-tax) in full, and on time.

THE MILLER: The Miller is a big-boned, brawny bull of a man. At wrestling he always wins the prize. He could yank a door off its hinges or, if need be, break it down by butting it with his head. With a broad, red beard, and a hairy wart on his nose (which has wide, black nostrils), he makes an ugly appearance. The sword and buckler at his side complete the picture of a man you wouldn't want to meet in a dark alley. When he opens his mouth it is usually to tell dirty stories. Wearing a white coat and a blue hood, he plays the bagpipes to escort the pilgrims out of town.

THE MANCIPLE: A manciple was a purchasing agent for a large institution. This one happens to work for a company of lawyers. Yet for down-to-earth cunning and shrewdness none of them were any match for him—with all their learning. He manipulated the funds so cleverly that he managed to put aside a tidy little fortune for himself.

THE REEVE: A reeve held a managerial position on a large estate. Like the Manciple, this Reeve is a shrewd organizer and handler of money. He is a skinny, bad-tempered sort of fellow, with a close-cut beard, and hair cut straight around the head, level with his ears. All of his master's sheep, cattle, swine, horses, and poultry, were under the Reeve's control. So sharp and cunning was he that all the bailiffs, shepherds, and stable boys feared him like the plague. In his youth he had learned a trade—that of a carpenter.

> **COMMENT:**   The fact that he was a carpenter really adds nothing to the portrait. But it becomes important later, when the Miller tells a nasty story about a carpenter, and the Reeve feels that he has to get back at the Miller. There are similar details in other portraits, which Chaucer later brings into the story-telling.

The Reeve rides on a good grey horse named Scot. And though he carries a sword by his side it happens to be rusty, which may mean that the Reeve would pull in his horns when his bluff is called. His general nastiness is also suggested by the fact that he rides alone, trailing behind the other pilgrims.

THE SUMMONER: As his name implies, the Summoner called offenders before the Church courts. This one had a fire-red face, such as you see in portraits of cherubim (angels). The Summoner was no angel, however. For one thing he was a confirmed lecher (given to sexual freedom). And he suffered from a disease which caused his hair, even his eyebrows, to fall out, and gave him hideous boils on his cheeks. Children shrieked when they saw him. And there was no ointment you could buy to clear up those boils. To make matters worse, he loved to eat garlic, onions, and leeks, and to drink strong, blood-red wine. He could spout a few words of Latin—enough to impress people—without really knowing what it meant. But when the chips were down he was a "hale fellow-well met." He'd do anything for a friend. For as small a gift as a quart of wine he'd look the other way, and let a fellow continue to enjoy his prostitute for another twelve months without reporting him. He also had the "ladies of the evening" under his thumb. At the moment, as Chaucer looks at him, he has put a huge garland of flowers on his head, and has made himself a shield out of a cake.

THE PARDONER: The Pardoner is the Summoner's saddle-mate. And they make quite a pair. A pardoner was a Church official who was permitted to cancel out a portion of the punishment due to certain sins, if the sinner made an appropriate offering.

> **COMMENT:**   It is obvious that the Friar, the Summoner, and the Pardoner were in a beautiful position to clean up a fortune, if they were at all dishonest. Unhappily, in Chaucer's day a very large percentage of them were dishonest. The Church was in need of a radical housecleaning.

The Pardoner had smooth, yellow, flowing hair. The curls spread down over his shoulders. He had a loud but high-pitched voice, and was beardless (in fact would never have a beard). The narrator imagines that he was a "gelding or a mare." All the details point to an example of a eunuch (a sexually undeveloped man). But as a Pardoner he is a huge success. He has a bagful of phony relics, which he palms off on the ignorant people. And in church he could sing an Offertory and preach a sermon which would loosen the tightest purse strings.

At this point Chaucer pauses in his description of the pilgrims, to ask his listeners and readers not to blame him personally for the stories which will be told. "After all," he says, "I am only reporting what was told to me, and I'm not very long on brains, anyway." He then goes on to describe the only remaining character, the Host, Harry Bailly.

THE HOST:

Harry Bailly is a large man, with deep-set eyes. He is forthright in speech, wise and well-bred, but above all, a very manly individual. To add to all of these fine traits, he has a merry manner about him. Harry takes over the pilgrimage from the start. "You are going all the way to Canterbury," he says, "and you are going to need some entertainment on the way." He proposes that each pilgrim tell two tales on the way to Canterbury and two on the way back. He will then judge the stories, and the pilgrim who has told the tale of "best sentence and moost solaas" will win the prize—a supper to be paid for by the rest of the journeyers.

> COMMENT: "Best sentence" means "having the most useful moral;" "moost solaas" means "the most entertaining." It is perhaps not so true today, but there have been many periods of history when literature was thought of as being good only if it had a useful lesson to teach. This is a principle to be kept in mind when reading some of the Canterbury tales.

Harry offers to be their guide as well as judge, and asks for unanimous agreement to his offer. It is granted.

CONCLUSION:

To celebrate their agreement the pilgrims call for wine. They go to bed promptly, since they must rise early the next day. At daybreak the Host rousts everyone out of bed, gathers them all together, and leads them out of town. After a short time he halts the group and prepares for the first tale. They draw straws, and the shortest straw falls to the Knight, so he must begin the story-telling.

> COMMENT: Since it is socially proper for the Knight to begin, Chaucer arranges it so that he gets the short straw. But the poet does not stick to a rigid scheme based on social priority. As the pilgrims ride along, he has the stories grow naturally out of arguments that spring up, or has tales relating to a single idea told in groups. As the pilgrimage proceeds, the order of the tales seems quite natural, in fact. Of course, the poem as it exists consists of a number of fragments and there are many gaps in the narrative. And Chaucer never did carry out his scheme to have each pilgrim tell four tales. Indeed, none of them except Chaucer himself tells more than one, and some never get to tell even one.

THE KNIGHT'S TALE

INTRODUCTION: The Knight's Tale is a romance of chivalry. Romantic story is customarily set in a faraway place and usually deals with extraordinary persons involved in strange or unrealistic events. "Chivalry," which comes from a French word for "horse," is a term for the entire set of customs and principles, and the code of honor connected with knighthood. It implied gentility, courage, and integrity. Even today the word "chivalrous" suggests the actions of a man who is decent, loyal, and brave in his behavior towards women. The Knight's Tale is a rather lengthy story, and some readers have felt that Chaucer meant it as a humorous reflection on the Knight's idea of what made up a good lively tale. Some of the details, too, like the notion that a prisoner, cooped up in a high tower, could fall in love deeply with a lady whom he can see only from a distance, seem wildly improbable. But it seems very unlikely that Chaucer would ridicule the Knight, and we must remember that what does not appeal to us may have appealed strongly to a medieval audience which had been trained to expect different things from a story. There are at least two important facts we must bear in mind in order to read this tale with appreciation:

1. A slow, leisurely narrative may not appeal immediately to a modern reader, accustomed to fast action and suspense; but life in the Middle Ages was lived at a much slower pace, and the literature frequently reflected this fact.

2. Elaborate description, with all sorts of colorful detail, was keenly pleasurable to people who lacked the kind of stimulation we take for granted—movies, television, and increasingly rapid transportation, for instance.

In any case the tale is clearly suited to the character of the Knight, both in subject matter and in the manner in which it is told. He is not only the primary representative of chivalry on the pilgrimage but he is himself a dignified and stately gentleman.

THE KNIGHT'S TALE: Once upon a time there was a duke named Theseus who was governor of Athens and a great conqueror. Returning to his city one day, he came upon a crowd of women, weeping and lamenting. The women (who were dressed all in black) begged him for pity, mercy, and aid. "We have all been queens or duchesses," they wailed, "but thanks to Fortune's wheel, we have become nothing but mean wretches."

> **COMMENT:** Medieval people tended to project the idea of success and failure in life's endeavors into the image of a great, turning wheel, presided over by a goddess named Fortuna. People from all walks of life could be sure of one thing—change was inevitable. The poor might become rich, the weak might become strong, but in the end Fortune's wheel would bring them low again. The question which became important in the face of such deadly certain change was: How should man react to the blows of Fortune? The Knight thinks of his story as providing an answer to this question.

The women went on to reveal that they had all lost their husbands at the siege of Thebes. Theseus, in truly chivalrous fashion, promised to bring vengeance upon the head of the tyrant Creon, who was responsible for their condition. Instantly, he turned his army around and set out for Thebes. Arriving at the city, he slew Creon, tore down all the walls and buildings, and restored to the unhappy ladies the bones of their dead husbands.

It happened, however, that Theseus' soldiers discovered among the Theban corpses two young knights, practically identical in appearance, named Palamon and Arcite. They were cousins, sons of two sisters. Just as quickly as he had granted mercy to the ladies Theseus dealt out justice to the two captives—imprisonment for life. Years passed, when one May morning a young maiden, Emelye by name, happened to walk in the garden below the tower in which Palamon and Arcite were slowly wasting away. It just happened also that Palamon, walking by the window, cast his eye upon Emelye whereupon he emitted a cry, as if he were stung to the heart. "For the love of God," said Arcite, "take it easy; there's nothing we can do about this imprisonment, we've got to put up with it." "It is not the prison," replied Palamon, "but that beautiful vision I see down there, the very image of Venus herself." At this Arcite decided to have a look for himself. His reaction was the very same. "I swear," he murmured, "if I don't at least have the chance to see that beauty at close range I am a dead man."

> **COMMENT:** What today we perhaps jokingly refer to as "love at first sight," was taken very seriously by people in Chaucer's day. It was imaginatively thought of as an attack by Dan Cupid—an arrow right through the eye and into the heart. How seriously Chaucer himself took the idea we may never know.

In what may strike us as a very impractical manner, Arcite and Palamon engaged in a violent argument as to who might be entitled to the hand of Emelye. (Neither of them, by the way, has the slightest idea of who she is, or even what her name is.) They both recall that they are blood brothers, sworn to assist each other, but quickly decide that in the case of love it is every man for himself. The argument in brief comes down to this: Palamon claims that Emelye is his because he saw her first; Arcite claims she is his because he loved her first (love in the only true sense, that is; he calls Palamon's feeling only a kind of spiritual affection).

The argument stretched out over a long period of time, but of course they both continued to languish in prison. It happened, however, that there was a visitor at the court of Theseus, a duke named Perotheus, who also happened to be a long-time friend of Arcite. He managed to have Arcite released—on one condition: if he were ever found in any country ruled over by Theseus he would be executed promptly, by decapitation. To listen to Arcite's complaints one would think that his plight was worse than before. Even in prison he at least had the chance to see Emelye once in a while. Now free, he was denied her sight forever. Just before leaving, Arcite launches into a long diatribe against Fortune, who has deprived him of the sight of his fair lady. But Palamon also sees himself in a more miserable condition than before. Arcite, he imagines, now has the opportunity to assemble an army, attack Athens, and marry Emelye.

COMMENT: This is a very remote possibility, the reader thinks, considering the character of Arcite. Chaucer certainly doesn't expect his readers to remain in suspense, wondering if Arcite will attack Athens. Palamon's speculations merely add to our sense of his own pathetic state.

The first part of the poem ends with the Knight's asking the question: Who indeed is worse off—Arcite or Palamon?

(Part Two) Arcite returned to Thebes, but after a year or two of sleepless nights thinking about Emelye he decided he had to return to Athens, even at great risk. Disguised as Philostrate he makes his way back to Athens, and is taken on as a page in the service of Emelye herself. His reputation for virtuous deeds and wholesome tongue grew so rapidly that in no time at all he became a dear friend of Theseus. Palamon, in the meantime, has spent seven more years in prison, and is practically out of his mind. As luck would have it, however, a friend finally helped him to break out of his confinement. He took to his heels in the dark but when day broke he had to hide himself in a grove of trees. Again by the most extreme outside chance, Arcite happened to be roaming about in the same grove in search of flowers for a May garland. Though he was still disguised as Philostrate he began to talk to himself, thinking he was alone, and to recite the whole history of his woeful state. Palamon, overhearing his confession, felt as if an icy sword had pierced his heart. He jumped out of hiding, cursing Arcite for the worst sort of traitor. Arcite threatened Palamon with death, but (recognizing the claims of the code of chivalry) promised to bring armor and weapons for Palamon on the next day. It was to be an equal combat. Arcite, returning the next day, engaged Palamon in fierce hand-to-hand battle, until they were ankle deep in blood. Chance (or Fortune) once more intervened in the person of Theseus himself. Being out on a hunt he had happened upon the very place where the cousins were fighting.

COMMENT: Modern readers may think that a story in which so many things happen by chance is a poorly plotted tale indeed. But this is Chaucer's very point. The operations of Fortune <u>do</u> have a random, accidental way of working themselves out. How can we put up with such a poorly constructed universe? This is one way of phrasing the main question which the poem presents.

In spite of the fact that Palamon has broken out of prison, and in spite of the fact that Arcite has violated the condition of his freedom, Theseus generously ("chivalrously") agrees to let them fight it out—but in the proper fashion. A year hence, they were both to appear with a hundred knights at their back, for a full-fledged tournament. The winner would have the hand of the fair Emelye in marriage.

(Part Three) Theseus spent the year preparing a great stadium in which the tournament was to take place. It was a mile in circumference, and on the eastern gate there was built an altar to Venus (Goddess of Love) and on the western gate an altar to Mars (God of War). Northward, in a turret on the wall, was placed an altar to Diana (Goddess of Chastity). All of these altars were richly decorated with statues and paintings, telling the stories of the gods as they are preserved in the old-time mythologies.

Theseus spared no expense to make the stadium as rich and fine as he thought such an important tournament deserved. As the day arrived for the jousting to begin Palamon and Arcite arrived with their followers— two hundred proud warriors in all. Theseus received them graciously into his palace, and wined and dined them in glorious fashion. There was rich food, heady wines, dancing, singing, and minstrelsy—truly a magnificent feast.

> **COMMENT:** The Knight obviously relishes the richness of detail. It is just the sort of magnificence and display to which a man of his station would be accustomed. This is the "good life" from the point of view of a medieval knight.

In the hours of darkness before the day of battle Palamon arose and went to pray before the altar of Venus. He asked not for victory or fame, but only to have possession of fair Emelye. If this was not to be, then he would prefer to be run through the heart with Arcite's lance. Just at daybreak Emelye herself arose and went to the altar of Diana to pray. She asked only that the fires of love be extinguished in Palamon and Arcite or, failing that, that she be given as a husband the one who truly loved her best. Diana appeared, and said that she was destined to become the wife of one of the two knights—who, she could not disclose. Shortly after this Arcite went to the altar of Mars. His prayer was simply for victory in the tournament. All of this occasioned quite a to-do among the gods and goddesses in heaven, until Saturn (the god of mysterious, fatal occurrences) put an end to argument. To Venus he promised that Palamon would win his lady; to Mars he promised that Arcite would be victorious in battle.

> **COMMENT:** If there is any suspense at all in the story it is from curiosity as to how these details will be worked out. Again, the answer is to be found in the thoroughly mixed-up way in which Fortune deals out the cards.

(Part Four) As the tournament was about to begin Theseus invented some additional rules. This was not to be a battle to the death; hence, poleaxes, daggers, and short swords were prohibited. And if either leader were to be captured, or if he fell in the fray, the tournament would immediately be at an end. Lines were drawn up—a hundred facing a hundred. Trumpets sounded. Horses and riders raced across the field. Then—a splintering crash. Knights picked themselves painfully off the ground, and paired off in single combat. Swords bit deep, and blood ran thick. When the confusion of battle cleared away, Palamon lay seriously wounded. Theseus declared the tournament to be at an end, and offered Emelye to Arcite as the winner. But suddenly, as Arcite was racing across the field to claim his prize, a miraculous thing occurred. His horse bolted and threw him to the ground. No medicines, no surgery, no prayers, could suffice to bring about his recovery. After making his peace with Palamon, and offering Emelye to him for his bride, the noble Arcite passed away. The funeral rites for Arcite were just as rich and fine as the tournament itself.

> **COMMENT:** The Knight is as painstaking in giving all the details of the funeral arrangements as he is in describing the stadium, and the tournament itself. Among other things this reflects the fact that color, figure, gesture, and strange ritual are quite as important to a romantic story as the plot itself.

The Knight's Tale ends with a long philosophical speech by Theseus, in which he explains that although life in this world seems haphazard and illogical, there is a God (he calls him the "Prime Mover") who sees things in a more complete way than humans do. There is order, and there is logic, but as mere creatures we are not always able to perceive it. The final note is a happy one, as Palamon and Emelye take each other's hand in marriage.

THE MILLER'S TALE

INTRODUCTION: The Miller's tale of Absolon, Nicholas, and Alisoun is Chaucer's version of a fabliau, or story about common characters involved in gross, frequently indecent events. There are some sub-literary examples of the type which are coarse in the extreme, but Chaucer's tale, while it is earthy in its humor, is certainly not obscene, and it makes an entertaining contrast to the very proper chivalric romance just related by the Knight. For one thing, Chaucer deals with the so-called "facts of life" in such an unembarrassed and healthy fashion that only the most puritanical conscience could find fault with his tale. And in any case the purely literary qualities of the poem are so magnificent that the reader is not invited to dwell on the more sordid pointedness of the various acts of retribution. Like many another great artist Chaucer has the ability to present a picture of sinners, knaves, and fools, without committing himself to a sympathetic attitude toward the vice they exemplify. Of course, he rarely condemns his characters but in this case the men, at least, are given suitable punishments for their wayward acts—a rather disgusting kiss, and a painful branding where we may be sure it did the most good. The tale is very appropriate to the character of the Miller, who, as we have seen, is a gross mountain of a man, constantly drunk and given to reciting lewd stories.

THE MILLER'S PROLOGUE: After the Knight's very refined (though somewhat tedious) story, all the pilgrims, especially the gentle-folk, praise him highly and observe that it is a fine story to bear in mind. The Host then calls on the Monk for a story with which to repay the Knight.

> **COMMENT:** The idea of "paying back" the previous teller is one device which keeps the stories moving along. We must remember, too, that the story-telling is a contest, for which the prize is a dinner at the common expense.

But the Miller, so drunk he can hardly sit astride his horse and swearing a blue streak, interrupts, saying: "By God, I know a "noble" tale with which I can pay back the Knight." At this point the Host, fearing the worst, tries to shush him up but is unsuccessful. The Miller hereupon announces in an alcoholic stammer that he is going to tell about a clerk, a carpenter, and a carpenter's wife. The Reeve, who had once been a carpenter, could see that he was about to be subjected to insult, so he bellowed a protest. But the Miller persisted in telling his story.

THE MILLER'S TALE:
There was once a rich old carpenter who used to take in boarders; usually, these were clerks (university students). At the moment there was with him a clerk named Nicholas. He not only knew a good deal about astrology, but he had been doing some extracurricular study on the subject of love. To complicate things, the carpenter had a young wife, Alisoun, of whom he was very jealous.

> **COMMENT:** The old husband who has been foolish enough to marry a young wife is a frequent character in comic literature. Invariably he becomes a cuckold (a man whose wife has been unfaithful). Some of the pleasure of reading such a story derives from the novelty the author gives to the old motif.

To make matters worse Alisoun was a farm girl who had been generously endowed with good looks and was in all respects physically attractive. (Chaucer goes into some detail in describing Alisoun's country charm.) She is gay, bright, prancing like a colt, full of vitality. One day, when old John the carpenter was away, Nicholas (who believed in the direct approach) went up to Alisoun and made some very improper advances. "Please take your hands away," said Alisoun, "or I'll scream" (though the tone of her voice was most unconvincing). Nicholas was a very effective suitor, however, and it was no time at all before they had conspired to put one over on John. Nicholas was so happy in anticipation that he played a tune on his fiddle. Soon after, Alisoun happened to be in church, where she came under the watchful eye of another clerk—a parish clerk named Absolon. Absolon was a very dainty individual, very particular about his dress and extremely feminine in his manner. Wearing scarlet trousers, and with intricately carved buckles on his shoes, he made a very elegant figure. (It is obvious that the Miller is vastly amused at this picture of someone so unlike himself.) The crowning touch in the portrait, from the Miller's standpoint, is this: Absolon becomes quite upset about people who break wind in polite company.

> **COMMENT:** The name Absolon (or Absalom) suggests a feminine kind of beauty. Absalom was a biblical personage known for his long golden hair. Moreover, Chaucer does not bring in the subject of breaking wind just for the sheer sake of vulgarity. As it later develops, this is the immediate cause of the final catastrophe in the tale. The plot of the story, the cause and effect relationships, and the assignment of punishments are all worked out with great rigor.

As it happens, Absolon complicates the love affair of Nicholas and Alisoun even further by going each evening to the bedroom window of John and his pretty wife, and singing love songs to the accompaniment of a guitar. John is so benighted that he sees nothing unusual about this, so Absolon continues his wooing—with songs, love-notes, messages carried by go-betweens, and a variety of gifts. But while Absolon wore himself out with wooing, Nicholas had the inside track. Finally, with John out of town one day, the lovers came to an agreement. Nicholas would stay in his room until John's curiosity got the better of him. Everything went by design. After two days the carpenter, thinking the clerk must have died, broke down the door and burst into the room only to find Nicholas gaping into space like a maniac. "His astrology has made him mad," gasped John, "I knew it was going to happen. For the love of God," he screamed, "come back to your senses." At length Nicholas stirred slightly and groaned something about the end of the world. Upon further prodding (and after swearing the carpenter to silence) Nicholas revealed a great secret. Through astrology he had discovered that on the following Monday a great rain would fall. It was to be greater than Noah's flood, and the entire world would be drowned in less than an hour. The poor carpenter was utterly beguiled.

> **COMMENT:** By having John taken in by Nicholas' astrology, and actively cooperating with him in a fantastic scheme to save their lives, Chaucer makes the carpenter more of a comic figure. It is more amusing to see foolish people bring about their own discomfort, than to have them made mere victims.

The old man pleaded with the clerk for some hope of salvation, at least for Alisoun. Nicholas pointed to the example of Noah, who, in similar circumstances, built a great ark. But he convinced John that a simple wooden tub would suffice for each of them. "I will save your wife," he promised, "have no fear of that." He then explained that the three tubs were to be suspended from the ceiling by ropes, and that each occupant was to be provided with an axe (to cut the ropes, leaving the tubs free to float). Wailing and complaining, John told all this sorry story to his young wife (who managed to act surprised, though she knew all the details better than he).

Regretfully but carefully the carpenter got the necessary tubs and fitted them out with provisions—bread, cheese, and ale, enough for a day. On the appointed Monday, as it drew towards evening, John, Alisoun, and Nicholas all climbed into their respective tubs. John fell into a fretful sleep, deep enough, however, to prevent his spying Alisoun and Nicholas climbing down their ladders to keep a long postponed meeting. Meanwhile, back at the parish house, Absolon had been keeping a lonely, all-night vigil. Thinking that John was away, he arose early in the morning while it was still dark. Dressed in all his finery he appeared at the customary bedroom window and called out for Alisoun.

> **COMMENT:** The language that Chaucer has Absolon use at this point is very delicate and refined. It increases our apprehension that some dreadfully vulgar fate is in store for him.

Alisoun, quite honestly, replied that she was in love with someone else, and that if he knew what was good for him he would go away and let her sleep. Absolon insists on a kiss, however. This proves to have been unwise. She did agree, finally, to one kiss, but in the darkness extended the wrong end of her anatomy (the rear end) out the window to the kiss-starved clerk. In a very short time Absolon discovered the hideous error he had made. In no time at all he was cured of his love-sickness. After coming to his senses Absolon (now free of delicate scruples) plans a fitting revenge. He goes across the street to a friendly blacksmith and borrows a red-hot poker. Returning, he pretends to want another kiss. Since this is too good an opportunity for Nicholas to pass up he presents _his_ rear end to Absolon, who is again waiting in the dark outside the window. "Speak to me, my fair dove," croons Absolon, at which (says Chaucer) Nicholas made a very vulgar noise— like a stroke of thunder. Absolon was almost caught off balance but this time was ready with the hot iron, and applied it vigorously to the mid-point of Nicholas' buttocks. "For God's sake! Help! Water! Water!" screamed Nicholas in anguish. His exclamations, of course, awakened the carpenter, ready for the first indication of a flood. With his axe he cut the rope and of course the tub went clattering down to the floor. For his folly the carpenter received a broken arm to add to the woe of being a cuckold.

> **COMMENT:** Poetic justice (fitting punishment) is awarded to John, Absolon, and Nicholas. For all his jealousy and watchfulness, John's wife was enjoyed by another man. For all his delicacy, Absolon was made to kiss someone's rear end. And for all his devious and roundabout scheming, Nicholas received a very direct jab with a scalding iron.

THE REEVE'S TALE

INTRODUCTION: The Reeve's Tale, since it so closely resembles the Miller's, requires very little introduction. It too is a fabliau. There is, however, a difference of tone and scope. The Miller's Tale has an uproariously funny plot, it is true, but it also happens to ridicule some of the "niceness" of refined love—what Chaucer called "fyn lovyng"— which the Knight has spoken of so sympathetically. The Reeve's Tale, on the contrary, seems to exist more for its own sake. It is little more than a nasty rejoinder by the Reeve to the insult he fancies he has gotten from the Miller. It is, of course, well adapted to the morose character of the Reeve—in fact, the tale extends the characterization of the Reeve.

> **COMMENT:** This reminds us of the twofold connection between tales and their tellers. Initially we judge each tale in terms of the excellence of its conformity to the character's portrait in the General Prologue. But the poem is a constantly growing thing. Tales are like speeches in the mouth of a dramatic character. We are continually forced to make new judgments about motivation and characterization.

THE REEVE'S PROLOGUE: Everyone laughs at the "nice" tale of Absolon and Nicholas but Oswald, the Reeve. His sullenness and anger are due not only to the fact that the Miller told his tale about a carpenter, but also to the fact that the carpenter was an old man. For Oswald is old, and the sands of life have almost run out. It is this more than anything which makes him angry. "Everybody knows," he says, "that when a man no longer has the ability to do a certain thing, he spends his time talking about it. Well, I'm no exception." There are only four sparks left in the ashes of old age he believes: Boasting, lying, anger, and covetousness. Except for these, what is left but senile decay? The Host gets impatient at the Reeve's sermonizing, and pratically commands him to tell his tale. Oswald agrees, but warns that he is going to use the same rough language the Miller used.

THE REEVE'S TALE: There was once a proud miller dwelling at Trumpington. (Like any number of millers he was also a thief.) His pride was due partly to his profession, partly to the goods he had managed to acquire in life, but most of all to the wife he had snared. She was the daughter of the town parson (presumably illegitimate), and she had been raised in a nunnery.

> **COMMENT:** The miller is a social climber. His wife is a status symbol. The joke is, that she is really not much to be proud of.

The wife is as good as the miller in putting on the dog. Among other things she is proud of her two children—a girl of twenty, and a six-month old baby. Now, the miller had been doing the grinding of grain for one of the colleges at Cambridge, and since the manciple had fallen ill the miller had become an outrageous thief, stealing a hundred times more than he had ever taken before.

One day, two of the Cambridge scholars who liked a good time prevailed upon the warden of the college to let them go to the mill to see the grain being ground. John and Alan were their names. Arriving at the mill, they joked with Simon, the miller, and asked him to let them watch the grinding process. Simon joked in return, but secretly decided to put one over on them, and steal even more than before. He had the typical middle-class scorn for the college-educated man, and he was going to enjoy pulling the wool over their eyes. Stealing out behind the mill, he loosened the bridle of the scholars' horse and sat back to enjoy the fun. When the grain was all ground and put in sacks John noticed that the horse was gone. The two scholars took off in hot pursuit and while they were gone the miller helped himself to half a bushel of their grain. They didn't get back until nightfall, and of course they knew what to expect so they didn't make an issue out of the missing grain. They simply asked to be put up for the night. The miller was going to rub it in, so he said: "I know how you college boys can prove with your logic and your syllogisms that a twenty-foot space is really a square mile. Let's see if you can turn this cottage into a hotel for the night."

> **COMMENT:** Comic characters frequently are caught in ironic statements. As we later learn, the scholars make the house do very well indeed, to the great chagrin of the miller himself.

Enjoying his great success, the miller decided to send into town for some bread and ale, and a roast goose. After drinking a plentiful amount the miller went to bed, snoring like a horse. There was only one bedroom in the house, however, so they were all in it, like one big, happy family. The miller and his wife were in one bed, with the baby's cradle at the foot. The daughter was in another bed, and the two young scholars in a third. Father, mother, and daughter were soon playing a symphony of snores, while Alan and John lay awake wondering how to get revenge on the thieving miller. Suddenly, Alan arose and went to the daughter's bed. For whatever reason (the Reeve doesn't speak too plainly here), whether Alan had known the daughter before, or whether she was simply taken unawares, the daughter made no outcry. Alan was set for the night. John did not wish to be outdone, however. So he cautiously pulled the baby's cradle over to the foot of his own bed. Sure enough, in a short time the wife arose to answer a call of nature. Returning, she was about to enter her own bed when she noticed the absence of a cradle. "Good lord," she exclaimed, "I almost got into bed with the clerk." Feeling around for the cradle, the wife got her bearings (as she imagined) and fell right into bed with John. John wasted no time, and if the wife was surprised (for the miller was twice John's age) she uttered no complaint.

This jolly life lasted until dawn. As Alan prepared to go back to his own bed, the daughter told him where he could find the cake she had made with the stolen grain. Of course Alan looked for the bed without the cradle, jumped in, shook his pillow-mate roughly (the miller, naturally) and told him of his huge success. The miller jumped up cursing, and there was a free-for-all such as the house had never seen. The miller was well beaten by Alan, and in the fracas got a crack on the skull from a stick his wife was wielding. Alan and John got off scot-free.

COMMENT: One of the main objections to this tale is not merely the general nastiness, but the feeling that there is really an excessive punishment meted out to the miller. "A trickster will himself be tricked," is the Reeve's summation of the story. But the tale seems to go to rather extreme lengths to illustrate that proverb.

THE COOK'S TALE

INTRODUCTION: Actually, there is no "Cook's Tale." What we have is a prologue and a very short fragment—so short, in fact, that it is almost futile to speculate about what the complete tale might have been like. One thing is certain. The Cook, Roger of Ware, was going to try to outdo the Reeve in sheer bawdy jesting. We do not know, either, why Chaucer interrupted his composition of the Cook's Tale. A likely guess, however, is that he realized that another tale like the Miller's and the Reeve's would be overdoing things. One who had read no further in Chaucer's poetry might come away with a very wrong impression of the poet, who is in reality a highly moral author (though no moralist).

THE COOK'S PROLOGUE: The Cook has been so delighted by the Reeve's tale, that he has been pounding Oswald on the back, even before he came to an end. "God forbid," he exclaims, "that we stop at this point. If you'll bear with me for a little while, I'll tell you a story that'll curl your hair. Believe me, it really happened." The Host breaks in, saying, "Make it a good one, Rog. God knows, you have a debt to pay to pilgrims. You've sold them enough re-heated pies, and flea-bitten parsley."

COMMENT: Harry quickly assures Roger that he is only joking. We soon realize that this camaraderie spiced with insult is only Harry's way of prodding the pilgrims into telling their tales.

THE COOK'S TALE: There was once a young apprentice in our city (Roger begins), a short fellow, brown as a berry, with neatly combed black hair. He was a good dancer and was known as Perkin Reveler. In fact, at bridal feasts, or any place where there was dancing, he was the life of the party. And when he wasn't dancing he was off gambling. His master put up with his escapades for a long time, but finally decided that one rotten apple could spoil the whole barrel. So he gave him notice. And good riddance, he thought. Perkin was not the least bit dismayed. He sent his bed and his clothing to a friend of his, a fellow just like himself. This friend had a wife who, for the sake of appearances kept a shop, but who actually playing fast and loose. . . .(Here the tale breaks off).

COMMENT: This is also the end of an entire fragment of the total poem. Even at this point, however, a reader can perceive the outlines of a unifying design. It is the interweaving of personality and tale, the antithesis of plot against plot, the alternative glimpses of single areas of human experience, that combine to form an organically growing—a unified, if not a completed—poem. The following** fragment begins with the tale of the Man of Law.

THE MAN OF LAW'S TALE

INTRODUCTION: The Man of Law's Tale is about a woman who is named Constance, and who is, for all practical purposes, the very idea of constancy (firmness of purpose) in human form. This observation throws light on two aspects of the tale: it resembles a saint's legend (a common literary type); and, it is to some extent allegorical.

1. **AS A LEGEND:** Saint's legends were stories about saints, which may have been true, or partly true, or even wholly fictitious. Whatever the case, they were written to inspire simple people—to make them emulate the virtue they saw illustrated in the saint's behavior. Some of them were outrageously far-fetched, but their value was not in how realistic they were, but in how well they drove home the idea they were exemplifying. Of course Constance was not a saint, but she is saint-like in her fortitude, her suffering, and her forgiveness.

2. **AS AN ALLEGORY:** An allegory is a story in which ideas are given human form. If a character in an allegory is named "Despair,"

** The order followed here is that of the most popular and widely used text of the Canterbury Tales.

then his whole function is to show accurately how despair operates. The more the author makes him resemble a real flesh-and-blood human being, the less allegorical the story becomes. Constance suffers so willingly that she soon loses any semblance of individual humanity; this makes the tale distasteful to some modern readers. An appreciation of allegory may have to be cultivated. Medieval audiences, in fact, were quite accustomed to this literary form.

There does not seem to be any special suitability of the tale to the character of the Man of Law. It might have been told by any pilgrim who was not a thoroughgoing scoundrel.

THE WORDS OF THE HOST TO THE COMPANY:

This section is a head-link. First, there are references to the position of the sun in the sky, which show that Chaucer thought of his stories as being told at very definite times on definite days. (Of course, the details were never worked out in a totally satisfying fashion.) The Host then addresses the Man of Law in what he thinks is legal language, and asks him to tell a tale.

> **COMMENT:** Actually, Harry asks the Man of Law to submit to his "judgment," after he has finished the tale. The joke here is that the lawyer is himself a judge—a court judge.

The Man of Law now reels off a catalogue of heroines who have been celebrated in story, whose lives he would like to recount except for the fact that Chaucer has already used them up. (Chaucer may be simply making a humorous allusion to his own prolific talent.) Finally, he begins.

THE PROLOGUE OF THE MAN OF LAW'S TALE:

The prologue is a sarcastic condemnation of poverty and praise of wealth. The Man of Law quotes a number of old saws, such as: "It is better to be dead than poor;" and, "When poverty flies in the window, respect flies out." He then congratulates rich merchants for their prudence in hoarding up wealth. The whole thing is only loosely connected with the tale itself, and it may simply have been Chaucer's intention to start an argument between the Man of Law and the Merchant.

THE MAN OF LAW'S TALE: (Part One)

Certain Syrian merchants, visiting Rome, were greatly impressed with the virtues of Constance, the Emperor's daughter. When the Sultan heard about her he decided he had to have Constance as his wife. His counsellors advised against it for many reasons, chiefly because of the difference in their religions. But the Sultan was so in love with the girl, simply from the reports he had heard, that he determined to become a Christian so that he might be her husband. Emissaries traveled back and forth, treaties were arranged, and the marriage plans formulated. Constance, of course, was not consulted about her own feelings. Like a dutiful daughter she prepared for the journey to Syria. But she wept and lamented, feeling indeed like an abandoned wretch.

> **COMMENT:** "Arranged" marriages were common in the Middle Ages (Romeo and Juliet is based on this idea, for example), and children, while they may have objected, had to submit.

but here, in the wedding of a Roman Christian girl to a Mohammedan Sultan of Syria, we have a really extreme case. Constance's complete submission to the will of her parents is an extraordinary example of fortitude.

As the ship bearing Constance to Syria was on its way, and the Sultan was preparing the wedding feast, the Sultaness (his mother) was making other plans. Angered that her son was giving up the old religion, she called a secret council. They all agreed to pretend to embrace Christianity, but at the climax of the feasting to fall upon the Christians and slaughter them. (The Man of Law, at this point, passionately decries the actions of the Sultaness. Among other things he compares her to the Serpent of Hell).

(PART TWO) The ship filled with Christians arrived at Syria. First, there was a triumphal procession, followed by days of revel and merrymaking. The time for the wedding feast had arrived. (The Man of Law interrupts his story again, this time for a condemnation of "unexpected woe," which always follows close upon the heels of happiness.)

COMMENT: These outbursts by the Man of Law do not really advance the story, but they underline for Chaucer's audience the point the story is supposed to be making.

The feast had hardly begun, when the Sultaness and her forces attacked, killing the Christians and all the Syrians who had allowed themselves to be converted. Constance, however, was set adrift in an open boat, without a rudder and without provisions. She put herself in the hands of God and became thoroughly resigned to her fate. For years the boat drifted from sea to sea, never catching sight of land. Why was she not drowned in the sea? How did she survive without food and drink? For an answer, the Man of Law points to the examples of Daniel in the lion's den, Jonah in the belly of the whale, and Mary of Egypt living in caves and deserts. He Who protected them, protected her.

Finally, the boat was cast up on the coast of Northumberland. Taken in by a castle-warden and his wife Hermengild (both pagans), Constance, by her example and through her miraculous cure of a blind man, converted them both. But Satan, envious of her success, plotted her downfall once more. A young knight of the town, madly in love with Constance, was rejected by her. He cut the throat of Hermengild and framed Constance for the murder. Brought before the king, Alla, Constance was a forlorn figure—no champion was there to defend her. But just as the knight was swearing on a bible that Constance was the guilty one, a mysterious hand struck him down. Falling forward, his eyes burst out of his face. Alla, converted by the miracle, took Constance as his wife. In due time she gave birth to a boy. Again, through vicious plotting, she was brought to misery. While the king was away he was told that Constance had borne a monstrous child. Mother and son were set adrift in an open boat, but through all adversity Constance never lost her faith in God and his ways.

(PART THREE) As Constance's boat touched shore in a heathen land a thief jumped aboard to rob and assault her. He fell overboard and was drowned. Meanwhile, the Roman Emperor had just heard of the slaughter of the Christians in Syria, and had sent a senator with an army to take revenge. The victorious senator, returning by sea, encountered the boat bearing Constance (though he had no idea of her identity)and carried her back to Rome with the young boy—Maurice was his name—to live in his own house. In the meantime, King Alla, repenting of his rash deeds, made a pilgrimage to Rome to seek forgiveness of his sins. In an accidental meeting with Maurice one day, Alla recognized his wife's feature's in the boy's face. Following him home, he was joyfully reunited with Constance. At a royal dinner party for Alla, the Emperor recognized his long lost daughter, and a tearful celebration took place. Maurice became the next emperor of Rome.

COMMENT: The injustices offered to Constance are incredible. The interruptions by the Man of Law seem annoyingly long and frequent. The various reunions are almost totally accidental. Above all, Constance's fortitude is unbelievably firm, and obviously endless. These objections, however, could not have existed for Chaucer's audience. The story is not meant to be realistic. It illustrates ideal behavior, and is not concerned with actual people and ordinary events.

HE EPILOGUE OF THE MAN OF LAW'S TALE: The Host compliments the Man of Law; then, swearing an oath, he calls on the Parson for a tale. The Parson (perhaps in jest) rebukes Harry for his swearing, and Harry (also jesting) calls him a Lollard (a term of rebuke, such as "Puritan" became in the Elizabethan period). The fragment breaks off shortly after, and there is some doubt about Chaucer's intentions concerning the next teller.

THE WIFE OF BATH'S TALE

INTRODUCTION: The third fragment consists of the tales told by the Wife of Bath, the Friar, and the Summoner. The Wife of Bath's Tale is distinguished by having a prologue which is practically twice as long as the tale itself. Moreover, there is a sense of urgency about it and a kind of breathless rhetoric that makes the prologue one of the most dramatic elements in the entire Canterbury Tales. For centuries moralists and theologians had been constructing a picture of woman and her place in the world which hardly accorded with the facts. Woman was the Devil's ally—a sensual and deceitful creature who was a constant occasion of sin and the cause of most of man's misfortunes. In the Wife of Bath Chaucer has created a ludicrous magnification of these complaints; she is a woman who freely admits to all the lust, the conniving, and the self-seeking which has been attributed to her, and who glories in the fact that she has thus been able to gain the mastery of her numerous husbands. Her prologue begins the so-called "marriage group" of tales, in which various aspects of the relationship between a man and his wife are explored through the fictions of several of the pilgrims. The Wife's specific point concerns the issue of lordship or dominance on the domestic front. Who should have the "maistrye" in a well-conducted marriage? The prologue is a humorous revelation of the tricks she used to gain the mastery over her five husbands, and her tale is a romance about an Arthurian knight who loses the "maistrye" to his wife but thereby gains an unexpected but blissful future.

THE WIFE OF BATH'S PROLOGUE: The Wife begins by announcing her allegiance to the rule of "experience" rather than that of "auctoritee."

> COMMENT: "Auctoritee," (or "authority") stands not so much for legal sway or power as it does for the opinions of older writers. (The idea has some connection with the fact that any writer of treatises or formal fictions is called an author. In a real sense ideas originate with him.) Of course there was far too much reliance on this sort of authority in the Middle Ages, and when such authority was responsible for the grotesque distortion of woman's character and place in society that it encouraged it invited satirical attack. The Wife's entire prologue is thus a sarcastic condemnation of some of the more naive theories about love in marriage. Merely by being the lively and robust performance which it is it lampoons the crabbed schematism of any number of ascetic moralists.

The Wife also pledges her fealty to the biblical injunction to "increase and multiply," and indicates her sympathetic understanding of a number of biblical accounts including Solomon's over-numerous wives and concubines, the command that a husband must leave his father and mother and cleave to his wife, and the Pauline observation that it is better to marry than to burn. The Wife is indeed a devil who can quote Scripture to suit her own ends. Virginity, she says, is merely advised, not commanded; a lord, after all, does not have all his household vessels made of gold—some are of wood. Virginity is therefore a great perfection but it is intended only for those who wish to live perfectly, "And," she remarks, "lordynges, by your leve, that am nat I." What principle can be deduced from the design of human organs of generation? Experience, once more, teaches that they were made "for office and for ese."

> COMMENT: "Office" means "the procreation of children." "Ese" is a euphemism for sexual pleasure. The Wife's statement is not so much an attack on the moral principle that procreation is the primary purpose of marriage, as it is a defense of the experiential truth that this is inevitably attended by pleasure. Some rather horrifying intellectual gymnastics were practiced by medieval thinkers in trying to make a clean separation between the two.

In short, the Wife says, she is a willing wife, the very opposite of those "daungerous" ("stand-offish") ladies of fashionable love poetry.

At this point the Pardoner interrupts, saying that he has been thinking of taking a wife, but that Dame Alice has talked him out of it. She threatens him with even more disturbing revelations about the state of so-called wedded bliss, and the Pardoner lets her get on with her tale.

The Wife now proceeds to describe her first three husbands, who were all old, rich, and physically weak. Once they had bestowed on her their lands and their wealth, she no longer had to study to gain their love, and she turned into a nagging shrew. She provides the pilgrims with a sample of her verbal attack on her defenseless mates (a one hundred and forty line monologue which raises a number of hypothetical accusations against wives and disposes of them with a magnificent show of logic-chopping). "If a woman is beautiful," (so she rages at them) "you say she is the prey of every lecher who passes by. If she is ugly you say she is ready to jump after the first man she sees. You complain about paying me compliments, and making a to-do over my birthday, but you are immediately suspicious if our hired boy (with the curly blond hair) happens to accompany me on a walk. You spy on me constantly, but I am telling you that not even Argus with his hundred eyes could be a bodyguard for me against my will. You say a woman's love is like Hell, like barren land, like wildfire (the more it burns the more fuel it looks for). And you say that just as worms ruin a tree, so a wife destroys her husband." Thus did the Wife steal the offensive; and even though she was herself in the wrong she could bite and whine like a horse and manage to get her own way. Deceit, tears, and the knack of spinning (webs as well as cloth?) God gave to woman by nature. Abed or abroad Alice's husbands got no rest until she had gotten her way. But as soon as they submitted she was all sweetness. "After all, dear husband," she would say, "man is the more reasonable sex, and he must therefore be the more long-suffering. Do you want to have me all to yourself? Well then, I am yours—to the last atom.

The Wife's fourth husband, she goes on to say, was a playboy. But she was in the prime of life herself, and could overlook some amount of bad treatment. It does her heart good to think back on those days and remember "that I have had my world as in my tyme." But without actually being unfaithful to her fourth mate the Wife made him fry in his own grease simply by making him think she had been. Now he is dead and in his grave (not an elaborate grave, to be sure; that would only be waste). Dame Alice's fifth husband was an Oxford clerk—shrewd, domineering, and stand-offish by turns. Even during her fourth marriage the Wife found herself attracted to this clerk, Jankyn by name; and at the funeral procession she found it impossible to keep her eyes from wandering in his direction.

COMMENT: The Wife accounts for her lusty nature by attributing it to her horoscope, or the astrological figure under which she was born. She is "al Venerien" (Venus gave her her lust) and her heart is "Marcien" (stalwart or bellicose—from Mars). Her "ascendent" was Taurus (the Bull). The absurdity of such a hypothetical horoscope for a woman is countered by the almost genuine pathos of her lament: "Allas! Allas! that evere love was synne!"

In a brief month they were married (though at forty she was twice Jankyn's age). The honeymoon ended abruptly, however, when Alice found to her

chagrin that her spouse not only spent all his time with his nose in a book
but confined his reading strictly to anti-feminist literature and stories c
"wikked wyves."   The history of Heloise, the Parables of Solomon, the
Ars Amatoria of the cynical Ovid, and many more, he had bound up in a
single volume to which he devoted all his evenings. To add insult to
injury, he delighted to quote horrible examples at Alice, who was fas
losing her patience. One night, in a particularly mischievous mood, he
began to read aloud, beginning with the story of Eve and the apple, and
read his way through the tales of Dejanira, Xantippe, and Clytemnestra, an
through accounts of murderesses, poisoners, and magdalens. At the heigh
of his rhetoric, he declaimed: "A fair woman is like a gold ring in a sow'
nose." Strained to the breaking point, Alice grabbed three leaves out of th
book and dealt Jankyn such a blow that he fell backwards into the fire
Starting up like a lion, he dealt an answering blow and his wife was stretche
on the floor like one dead. (By playing possum Alices gets the advantage.
As Jankyn bent over her remorsefully, Alice hit him on the cheek an
pretended to resign herself to death. These maneuvers and Jankyn's sho
of emotion gave the Wife of Bath the "sovereignty" she desired. From tha
day forward, she was as kind and true to her husband as he was to her

THE WIFE OF BATH'S TALE: In olden days, a knight of the court o

King Arthur committed rape on the person of a young maiden. Justice wa
swift, and he was condemned to death. He would have lost his hea
summarily, but for the fact that the queen and her ladies-in-waiting sue
for his life. His case was left up to the queen to decide. "Your life is i
jeopardy," said the queen, "but you can be restored, if, at the end of
twelve-month, you can give me the answer to this question: 'What is
that women most desire?' "

The Knight searched everywhere, and received many answers none o
which (he was certain) was the right one. Riches, honor, dress, pleasur
flattery, attention, and liberty were all suggested to him. One ver
promising possibility was the answer that women desire to be judge
capable of keeping a secret. A legend of Midas, who importuned his wif
not to reveal that he had been given asses' ears, was offered in support o
this opinion. But the knight was sure he had not hit upon the answer, ar
his year was almost up. Riding through a forest, he happened upon
vision of four-and-twenty ladies dancing on a green. As he drew nea
however, the vision vanished, only to be replaced by the figure of an ug
hag. Overcoming his revulsion, the knight approached and the loathly woma
offered to aid him in his quest. After hearing his plight, the hag promise
him the answer he wished—on one condition. He would have to perfor
the next deed she required of him, if it lay in his power to do so. Glad
did the knight pledge his faith to the woman. Together they rode back
the court, where the ladies were assembled to hear his answer. Silen
fell over the courtiers as, in a manly voice, the knight pronounce
"Women desire to have sovereignty and mastery over their husbands
Neither wife, nor maid, nor widow could contradict this answer, a
his life was spared.

Suddenly the loathly lady started up and revealed to the assembled cou
the pact she had made with the knight. "I pray thee, Sir," she the
exclaimed, "take me for your wife." The knight answered, "Alas, I know
made such a promise, but for the love of God don't hold me to it. Ta
everything I own, but let my body go." It was all to no avail. No descriptio

of the wedding day is necessary (says the Wife) because it was all gloom and woe. Brought to bed with his new spouse, the knight could do naught but writhe in agony. "Do all husbands act like this," inquired the hag; "please tell me what is wrong and perhaps I can do something about it." Quite openly the knight revealed that it was her foulness, her age, and her low breeding which was the source of all his sorrow. The hag then delivered a lecture on truly good breeding, or "gentilesse," the import of which is that gentility is not a mere matter of appearances—"virtue is true nobility." As for the poverty, that is no great burden either; in fact, it can be the avenue to salvation, as pagan and Christian moralists both agree. Nor are her ugliness and age necessarily unfortunate, since her husband should at least have no fear of becoming a cuckold. "Foulness and old age are great guardians of chastity," she reminds him. Nevertheless, she was willing to compromise, and offered the knight a choice of two alternatives: to have her ugly and old but faithful until death; or to have her young and fair, and to take his chances on her fidelity. Faced with such grim alternatives the young knight put himself entirely in his wife's governance. As soon as it was apparent that she had gained the mastery, the wife relented and told her husband that he would be able to have her fair and good. He was in a transport of bliss, and they lived in perfect joy ever after.

> **COMMENT:** It is obvious that there is an excellent adaptation of tale to teller, in this case, and that the prologue makes the connection even more apt. The moral grotesqueness of the Wife (not to mention her manly appearance) makes a fitting parallel, it has often been noted, to the physical ugliness of the hag.

THE FRIAR'S TALE

INTRODUCTION: The Friar's Tale is a type of popular tale; it deals bluntly and vividly with the vicious misconduct of clerical office-holders, and it speaks from a point of view sympathetic to the frequently helpless victims of the lechery, greed, and callous unconcern of predatory churchmen. At the same time Chaucer adds to the plot an element of learned discussion of some nice theological points concerning the presence of demons in the world, and their power over human souls. This "scholastic" material continues the tone of academic exposition begun by the Wife of Bath in her professional analysis of a wife's prerogatives. The tale is well suited to the character of the Friar, and since it deals with a depraved summoner it calls forth a tale from the pilgrim-Summoner by way of rejoinder.

THE PROLOGUE OF THE FRIAR'S TALE: At the conclusion of the Wife's tale the Friar congratulates her on her probing examination of a very difficult matter, but announces his preference for less learned themes, and offers to tell a tale about a summoner. A summoner, as everyone knows (says the Friar), is a fellow who runs around handing out summonses to fornicators, and is beaten regularly on the outskirts of every town. The Host politely asks the Friar to refrain from insulting the Summoner, but the Summoner himself intervenes and asks that the Friar be allowed to go on, promising to pay him back in full measure.

THE FRIAR'S TALE:
Once there was an archdeacon who carried out his offices with great vigor, punishing fornication, witchcraft, bawdry, adultery, usury, simony, and a number of other ecclesiastical offenses, but he was most active in his punishment of lechers. He had a deputy at hand, a summoner, and a slyer boy was nowhere to be found in England. He had a private system of espionage, with paid informers. He could afford to spare a couple of lechers, if they could lead him to two dozen more.

> **COMMENT:** There is a strong implication that the intense interest in lechery on the part of both the archdeacon and the summoner is a perverse psychological manifestation of their own sense of guilt. When the Friar says, "For thogh this Somonour wood (mad) were as an hare, / To telle his harlotrye I wol nat spare," he is punning on the words "hare" and "harlotrye," and using the hare (a symbol of sexual license) as a characteristic of the summoner.

The summoner had a regular staff of wenches whose job it was to lure men—gentlemen and common fellows equally—into compromising situations. Then the summoner would take bribes from the men, and let the women go, pretending that he was doing it out of his good nature. In short, to seek out adulterers and illicit lovers was his whole intent.

It happened one day that he was on his way to force a bribe from an old woman, when he came upon a yeoman, dressed all in green. In a remarkably short time (because they had a strikingly similar outlook on things) they became sworn brethren. At the summoner's prompting the yeoman revealed that he was a bailiff, and he described his duties, which amounted to little more than extortion, tricks, violence, and ill-gotten gain.

> **COMMENT:** Of course the reader realizes that the description fits the summoner to a tee, and it is at this point that his apprehension increases as the summoner insists that the yeoman identify himself.

"Brother," said the yeoman, "I am a devil, and my dwelling is in Hell. I ride about the country looking for easy pickings, and you do the very same thing." The summoner was surprised, to say the least, but never lost his complacency. In fact he pressed the yeoman for details about his mission on earth. He replied that he was out to gain a human victim, and that as for reasons, well, suffice it to say that they were sometimes simply the instruments of God's justice. Without Him they had no power to act on earth. To the summoner's question, what sort of shape or appearance they had in their natural surroundings, the yeoman rather pointedly replied that he would soon be where he would not have to have the answer from him.

Upon entering a town, they saw a carter whose horses were stubbornly refusing to move. "The devil take you—horses, cart, hay, and all," cried the carter. At this the summoner (out of malice or mischief) whispered in the yeoman's ear and told him to go ahead and take the cart and horses. But the malediction was not spoken from the heart, as the yeoman explained, and so he had no power to remove them. Shortly after, they found themselves at the old widow's gate, whereupon the summoner shouted insults as a greeting, and demanded payment of twelve pence for acquittal of the summons he was about to present. The poor woman asked if she might answer the charges by proxy, since she was innocent of any wrongdoing. But the summoner continued his browbeating and insults, finally threatening to carry off the woman's new pan in payment of an old debt. Exasperated beyond all endurance, the poor widow screamed, "the Devil take your body and my pan both." At this the yeoman-devil asked her if she really intended her words, to which she replied that she did, unless the summoner were to repent of his false accusations. The summoner refused to repent and was carried off to Hell that very night. The tale ends with an imploration by the Friar that these summoners might become good men, and repent of their misdeeds.

THE SUMMONER'S TALE

INTRODUCTION: The Summoner's Tale is probably Chaucer's version of a popular story like the Friar's Tale, although no source for it is known to exist. The difference lies mainly in the fact that the Summoner's Tale, while it does not contain the sort of witty reference to obscene and immoral behavior seen in the Friar's Tale, does go beyond it in unabashed vulgarity.   The tale is overlaid with elements of academic discussion, however; in fact, the humor depends to a great extent upon the absurd misapplication of scholastic quiddities to the vulgar substance of the plot. The tale is well suited to the Summoner, and the two tales together provide an amusing sort of symmetry, and an impressively dramatic interlude as the pilgrims continue their riding "by the weye."

THE PROLOGUE OF THE SUMMONER'S TALE: The Friar's story of the diabolical summoner causes the pilgrim-Summoner to shake like an aspen leaf with rage. "This Friar boasts some knowledge of Hell," he exclaims, "and it is small wonder, considering the fact that friars and fiends are so closely related." He then tells of the friar who had a vision of Hell, and who remarked to his angel-guide on the absence of any friars down there.   The angel showed him millions of friars swarming from between Satan's buttocks like bees from a hive. Upon awakening from his vision that friar quaked with fear at the punishment which was to be his in the very nature of the fact that he was a friar.

THE SUMMONER'S TALE: In a section of Yorkshire a friar used to go about preaching and begging.   One morning he gave an especially moving sermon on the necessity of contributing to the construction of churches for friars to carry on their holy work of prayer. After leaving the church he made his way through town, begging goods or services at every door. At length he came to the home of a well-to-do townsman named Thomas, who happened to be bedridden with some illness. (The friar had been refreshed at his house many times in the past.) Thomas greets him with familiarity, and as the man's wife enters the friar greets her with even greater familiarity. He embraces her and kisses her, and chirps like a sparrow.

> **COMMENT:** There is a good deal of irony in the Summoner's account. For one thing he has the friar remark: "Glosynge is a glorious thyng, certeyn, / For lettre sleeth, so as we clerkes seyn." That is, "the letter killeth, but the spirit giveth life." To "gloss," or interpret Scripture to find its spiritual meaning is a necessary work; but "gloss" also means to "pull the wool over someone's eyes," and this, it is hinted, is exactly what the friar is trying to do to Thomas.

The wife complains that Thomas' trouble is largely due to his chronic anger, and the friar proceeds to give him a sermon on the bad effects of anger—replete with examples. But the wife first informs him that their child had died shortly after his last visit. The friar pretends that he and the entire fraternal community had had a vision of the child's death and his entrance into the blisses of heaven, and that they had all sung a Te Deum for his soul's rest (this, of course, to convince the woman that her offerings were money well spent). He then discourses on the virtues of poverty and fasting (outright hypocrisy from one who has just ordered the sumptuous meal the friar has requested from the wife), and he mentions Moses' fast of forty days, the abstinence of Aaron and the other priests of the temple, and even adduces the eating of the apple by Adam and Eve as an example of gluttony. From gluttony he moves on to riches, and the necessity of being "poor in spirit," of avoiding pomp and high living. Thomas has contributed heavily to the orders in the past, however, and he does not see that his illness is any just reward for his liberality. The friar's explanation is that Thomas has diversified his gifts too much, and watered down their efficacy. A bushel of oats here, twenty groats there, a penny to this friar, twopence to that one—what does it amount to? In his own words, "What is a ferthyng worth parted in twelve?" His conclusion, of course, is for the townsman to give all his money to the friar's own order.

The friar then resumed his sermon on anger, with a long introduction connecting anger with the Devil, the serpent, and with a vengeful woman. (This is ironic, as it turns out, for the friar is driven to angry expostulations by the indignity which is made to suffer.) He quoted the example mentioned by Seneca, of an angry king who brought about the death of three innocent men; of Cambises, who slew the son of one of his subjects in anger; and of Cyrus, who destroyed an entire river because his horse had been drowned in it. He followed up the examples with forceful persuasion but Thomas was not only unimpressed but simply made angrier by the friar's "false dissymulacioun." But he offered to give the friar everything which he had in his possession, if he would agree to swear an oath that every friar of his community would receive an equal share, and told him to put his hand down at his back to find what he had hidden away. The greedy friar, quickly agreeing, groped here and there finding nothing until the man broke wind. The friar leaped up in anger like a mad lion, and threatened Thomas with retribution. Going to the lord of that town, whose confessor he was, the friar told the whole story. The lord and his lady received the account with real (or perhaps with mock) solemnity, and the lord made a rather academic examination of the problems connected with carrying out the agreement—not without some admiration of the townsman's shrewdness in hoodwinking the friar.

The solution, however, came from the lord's squire who, as he was carving the meat, had overheard the entire matter being discussed. All that was needed, he decided, was a calm day, a cart-wheel (which had twelve spokes), and the thirteen members of the friar's community. Each of the other twelve would set himself to the end of one of the spokes, the friar at one end of the nave of the wheel, and Thomas, the beneficiary, at the other end of the nave, where he would simply repeat his earlier performance. The lord, his lady, and all the men present—except the friar—alleged that the squire had spoken as subtly as Euclid or Ptolemy. (Here another fragment ends.)

THE CLERK'S TALE

INTRODUCTION: The Clerk's Tale is a literary version of what is ultimately a folk tale involving a woman and an other-worldly lover. It seems to have been first put into strictly literary form by Boccaccio, though Chaucer acknowledges his immediate source to be a version by Petrarch. Just as the Man of Law's Tale extols the virtue of constancy, so this tale emphasizes the nobility of patience. All the difficulties inherent in the excessive idealization of the Constance story are present in a reading of the story of patient Griselda, and there are others as well. It is not so much that motivation is lacking as that Walter, Griselda's husband, is wantonly perverse, and it has been suggested that this difficulty is simply a result of successive modifications of the folk tale, none of which ever came to grips with the problem of realistic and convincing motivation. The Clerk, whose profession has suffered attack at the hands of the Wife of Bath, is in a sense replying to the Wife's vision of marital bliss. At the end of the tale, in fact, he specifically addresses himself to the Wife of Bath, "and al hire secte." The Clerk is something of an enigma, and it is difficult to be sure about the success with which the tale has been adapted to his character as we find it in the General Prologue. With its emphasis upon the virtue of patience, of course, and because of the generally elevated and dignified style, it is quite appropriate to the sort of mentality one might expect of the Clerk.

THE PROLOGUE OF THE CLERK'S TALE: The Clerk has been riding along lost in thought, and Harry Bailly interrupts his reveries. "This is no time for study and logical subtleties," he says, "tell us a merry tale. And save your rhetorical figures and decorations, and the high style of expression, for some time when you are writing. Speak plainly so we can all understand you." The Clerk humbly submits to the Host's demands, and offers to tell a tale he discovered in the works of Petrarch. After a short eulogy of Petrarch, and a description of Petrarch's opening lines, he begins.

THE CLERK'S TALE: (Part One)

In the land of Saluzzo, in Italy, there was a marquis who was lord of the country as his fathers had been before him. His subjects, of high and low estate both, were loyal and loving and he ruled in an atmosphere of calm and pleasure. This young lord, Walter by name, was a paragon of gentle breeding; he was fair, strong, discreet, and courteous. But he lived only for the present, spending his time in hawking and hunting, and, worst of all, had not as yet married. The people were afraid of being ruled by a successor not of Walter's blood, and they finally sent a delegation to beseech him to marry as soon as possible, offering to choose a wife for him, if he wished, one of the highest and most well-bred ladies of the land. The marquis agreed to take a wife—on two conditions: he was to choose her himself; and his people were to promise to worship her just as if she were an emperor's daughter. They all agreed to this, and Walter set the day for the wedding and commanded his officers to prepare the feast.

(PART TWO)

Not far from the palace was a small village whose people worked the soil for their livelihood. One of these poor souls was Janicula, who had a daughter, Griselda, fair enough to the eye, but in inner virtue the fairest under the sun. Poverty and hard work had left no room for lust and idle pleasure. Though young in she had a mature and serious understanding, and held her father in reverence and love. The marquis (unobserved) had seen her many times as he was out hunting, and had decided that if he were ever to marry it would be none other than Griselda—simply for the great goodness that was in her. The wedding day was approaching but the marquis had revealed his choice neither to his people nor to Griselda herself. On the morning of the appointed day he led his people in a rich procession to the little village where Griselda lived. Approaching her doorway, he asked if her father was at home, and, taking the old man aside, humbly asked his permission to marry his daughter. Janicula, in outright astonishment, told the marquis to govern the matter as he thought best. Walter then put the question to Griselda herself, but before receiving an answer, told her of the conditions she must agree to: to do his will cheerfully, even if it caused her pain; and never to grumble or frown at any command he might utter. This, Griselda agreed to. The marquis then presented her to his people, and amidst celebration Griselda was arrayed as a bride, and they were espoused.

> **COMMENT:** The Clerk puts a good deal of emphasis on the external glitter of the court and the lowliness and filth of Griselda's home and her clothing, to point up his theme that inner virtue is true nobility.

Griselda, virtuous always, simply increased in virtue as time passed; her eloquence, kindliness, and dignity endeared her to all her subjects and her fame spread so that people came from far and near to behold her. In short, her presence removed all discord, rancor, and sadness from the land. Not long after, Griselda gave birth to a daughter, and though a boy would have been preferred, this was at least proof that she could have children; they could hope that the next child would be an heir to the marquis' title.

(PART THREE) While the child was still very young the marquis had a sudden urge to put his wife to a test—to take the child from her, and see if she were able to live up to the compact they had made.

> **COMMENT:** From the standpoint of a modern reader, for whom the psychological analysis of motive is frequently the main point of a piece of fiction, this wanton act, which Chaucer is at no pains to explain (he simply allows the Clerk to say: "he ne myghte out of his herte throwe / This merveillous desir"), is a defect in the story. But it is the way of the fairy-tale, and is really no more destructive of enjoyment than many of the conventions we accept almost without being aware of them.

The marquis reminded Griselda at some length of her promise to him, and then commanded her to show her patience at work in submitting to his will. Griselda's answer ("my child and I are yours—do your will upon us") pleased Walter greatly, though he did not show this in his face. When a sergeant came to remove the child, Griselda demurred not at all, but asked only for the right to kiss it for the last time. And she implored the sergeant to bury the body where it might not be torn to pieces by animals or birds of prey. The sergeant then returned to the marquis and revealed all the details of Griselda's reactions. The child was sent to be cared for by Walter's sister, the Countess of Panik, near Bologna. Griselda continued as glad, as humble, as busy, as if nothing had ever happened.

(PART FOUR) Four years later Griselda gave birth to a boy. On the pretext that the people were murmuring against him because the blood of Janicula was going to succeed to his title, Walter repeated his earlier temptation of Griselda. The same ugly sergeant came in the same way; the same patience, the same final kiss; and the same request for decent burial. This child, too, was sent off to Bologna.

> **COMMENT:** At this point the Clerk allows himself some speculation about the possibility of such outrageous behavior as that which Walter has displayed. He concludes that there are indeed some people of such utter single-mindedness. Griselda seems equally single-minded, however, and it alerts the reader to symmetry between the wanton doggedness of Walter, and the sublime patience of Griselda.

When the daughter was twelve years of age the marquis decided upon one final temptation. He arranged a counterfeited papal permission to put away his wife Griselda and wed another. And he ordered his sister, the Countess, to bring the children home without revealing their identity. Plans went on apace for the celebration of another wedding.

(PART FIVE) Carrying out this final plot, the marquis announced to Griselda his decision to take another wife. He was not able, he informed her, to marry so far beneath his station, and his subjects were again grumbling against him. With patience and humility Griselda agreed to return to her father's house, and in a passage of lyrical intensity she declaims upon the theme: "Naked came I out of my mother's womb, and naked shall I return thither" (though she alters it, appropriately, to "father's house"). Wearing only a smock, bareheaded and barefoot, she returned to Janicula, who received her willingly (though in tears) and there she dwelt for a time. (The Clerk ends this part with an explicit comparison of Griselda to Job.)

(PART SIX)   As the children were arriving from Bologna, Walter sent for Griselda to prepare the palace for the wedding, on the pretext that she was more familiar than anyone with his desires. Griselda patiently returned and made all ready. As the (pretended) future bride passed along the way, the people all praised their lord's wisdom in choosing such a fair wife, one of such "heigh lynage."

> **COMMENT:** Using Griselda's own daughter as the imagined bride helps to underline the poem's subordinate theme of "judging by externals." And the Clerk now excoriates the "stormy peple" for their fickleness and lack of discretion.

(As the tale now draws near its climax Walter's open and cruel taunting of his wife rises in intensity.) Suddenly, however, Walter's desire to tempt his wife was sated. Taking Griselda in his arms he told her that he finally was convinced of her steadfastness; that the supposed "bride" was her own daughter, and that her son was also alive and destined to be the next marquis. All of these things, he asserted, he performed not out of malice but only from a sincere desire to prove her "womanhead." Griselda fell to embracing her children and Walter assuaged her sorrow and had her reinstated in the palace. They lived many years in peace and harmony; their daughter married a rich lord; Janicula was given residence in the palace; and the son succeeded to his father's marquisate and married well—though he put his wife through no such trials!

The Clerk reminds his listeners that no one expects wives to imitate the absolute humility of Griselda, but that everyone should be constant in adversity to the extent that he is able.

> **COMMENT:** The symbolic meaning to which the story has been pointing all along is here made explicit: "And for oure beste is al his (God's) governaunce. / Lat us thanne lyve in vertuous suffraunce."

With a genial jibe at the Wife of Bath, and a lyric "burying" of Griselda and her patience "bothe atones" the Clerk ends his tale.

THE MERCHANT'S TALE

INTRODUCTION: The Merchant's Tale contains a number of stock literary motifs, but it is hard to assign it to a specific classification. Nor is there a known source for the tale. The basic plot involves the figure of the aged lover (known in literary and dramatic criticism as the senex amans) who is destined to be deceived or cuckolded. There is a partially allegorical aspect to the tale, if only in the assignment of names: January (the old man) marries May (the young woman); his brethren and advisers are Justinus (the righteous man) and Placebo (the flatterer—literally, in Latin, "I will please"). It contains the device known to classical literature (and similar to that in the Knight's Tale) of an action among the gods paralleling that among the humans. The pear-tree episode with which the tale concludes is well known as a folk tale. But here, as in the case of the Nun's Priest's Tale, it is the inclusion of a great variety of miscellaneous allusion and the binding of these elements into a tightly organized structure that carries the true Chaucerian ring. It is well chosen for the character of the Merchant, and further adapted to his situation (as that is explained in his own prologue) by ironic comments alluding to the Merchant's recent marriage and the keen disappointment he has met. There is a painful and cynical frankness running through the poem, but considering the fact that it deals with adultery, and that there is even less to be said in extenuation of the folly of January and the infidelity of May than for old John and Alisoun of the Miller's Tale, it is a very successful performance.

THE MERCHANT'S PROLOGUE: The Clerk has ended his envoy (or postscript) by advising ugly wives to be free with their favors and to let their husbands worry, and weep, and wail. The Merchant begins by complaining that he has had enough of wailing, weeping, and worrying, and so have many other married men. He has a shrew for a wife, one who would be more than a match for the Devil himself. And there is a considerable difference between Griselda's patience and his wife's cruelty. He has been married only two months and he is convinced that he has a tale of woe that would outstrip the recital by a single man of the woes of a lifetime. The Host prevails upon the Merchant to recount at least a part of his marital "sorwe."

THE MERCHANT'S TALE: There was once a prosperous knight who lived in Pavia, and who had been for sixty years a wifeless man (though his fact had not interfered with his enjoying the freedom of a married man with women). Suddenly, after his sixtieth birthday, he had a desire to taste the blisses of wedded life. (The Merchant now puts in the mouth of the old man—and adds sarcastically in his own voice—a number of stock reasons for marriage: marriage is a paradise on earth; a wife is the fruit of a man's treasure; a man ought to have an heir; for "wele" or "wo" a wife will not forsake her husband, and so forth.) Continuing his sarcastic "praise" of marriage, he heaps superlative on superlative, the absurdity of his statements becoming more and more obvious, until he reaches the climactic question: "How myghte a man han any adversitee / That hath a wyf?"

> **COMMENT:** January's zeal for marriage we recognize as an instance of rationalizing a lustful desire. His reasons have a certain plausibility, but they have a valid application only to a man of younger years. As for the Merchant himself, his sarcasm is based on the fact (as he has just discovered) that no individual woman lives up to the impossible ideals man has set for her.

At this point the Merchant provides ironic examples of "good women"— Rebecca, Judith, Abigail, Esther (all of whom, in fact, brought some man to destruction)—and in a similar vein quotes Seneca, Cato, and the Bible, on the utility of wives. He then returns to his narrative of January. The old man called his friends together to announce his plans for marriage. The lady had to be young, both because he wished to have an heir, and because (though he was old in years) he was young in heart and needed a sympathetic wife. He got mixed advice from his friends, but the pros and cons were most ably summed up by his two brethren, Placebo and Justinus. Placebo felt that January had explained himself in such holy and serious terms that he could do naught but agree with him. Justinus counselled caution and thoughtful consideration of all the cares of marriage, but was dismissed as a foolish academic. All the others assented to his plan.

January spent some time turning over in his mind the merits of a number of young women dwelling nearby, and finally settled on one. Calling his friends together again to announce his choice, he posed a question which was bothering him: if marriage is a heaven on earth, and if the heaven of the life hereafter was to be bought with great tribulation, how was he to be sure of obtaining the reward that Christ had earned for him? Justinus, out of all patience, expressed the hope that he might repent of his decision to marry, or that failing that, his wife might prove to be no heaven on earth, but merely a purgatory. But even without a satisfactory answer to his dilemma January went ahead and was married with great solemnity. The joy of the wedding feast was indescribable (though January was beset by an impatience for his guests to leave) and everyone was filled with bliss but a young squire named Damian, who had become enraptured with May, and was almost dying of the pain of unrequited love. (But of this January had no knowledge.) He finally cleared the hall of guests, waited for the priest's blessing of the bed chamber, and then happily assumed the role of husband. In the morning he sat up in bed and sang aloud (like a bird), but while he sang the skin about his neck shook (also like a bird).

> **COMMENT:** The absurdity of January's foolish venture is most pronounced at this point. Chaucer emphasizes all the physical details of age as a background for the silly rationalizations of January.

Damian meanwhile had been languishing lovesick in his bed for four days before he was missed by January, who then suggested that May might pay the young squire a visit. Unseen by the women who accompanied her, Damian managed to pass a love-note to the young bride. At the first opportunity she read it, and then carefully destroyed it. May had taken a fancy to Damian, as it developed, and she wrote a letter in turn and during her next visit managed to slip it under his pillow. This gesture caused Damian to revive and resume his duties about the house.

Not the least of January's delightful diversions was a garden walled with stone—surpassing in its beauty the garden described in the Romance of the Rose. There was only one key, and this January kept under close scrutiny. But suddenly, at the height of his prosperity, January was struck blind.

> **COMMENT:** The use of physical blindness as a symbol of moral or intellectual limitation is of course a common literary device. Two notable examples occur in Sophocles' Oedipus the King and Shakespeare's King Lear.

To add to his foolishness in marrying at all, January now conceived an overwhelming jealousy of his young wife and would let her go nowhere without holding tight to her hand. By signs and gestures, however, she managed to communicate with Damian and after securing a wax impression of the sole key to the garden, gave it to him to be duplicated. Before too long, January had a desire to take the pleasures of the garden, and holding May by the hand he entered it (but not before Damian had let himself in with his own key). The squire, on a sign from May, climbed up the pear tree.

The day was bright, with a blue sky and a brilliant sun, and Pluto and his wife Proserpina were discussing the situation developing down below on earth. Because of the villainies and deceits of women, Pluto resolved to restore January's sight just at the moment when he might unmistakably perceive his wife's infidelities. Proserpina, because of the lechery of men, was equally resolved to provide May with a persuasive excuse. With January holding on to the bole of the tree, May climbed up to keep the assignation with her lover. At a crucial moment, as Pluto had promised, January found his vision restored, and set up a hue and cry at the sight that met his eyes. But May quickly convinced him that this was the only method she was able to hit upon by which she might restore her husband's sight. That he had seen any more than a "struggle" with a man (she soon convinced him) was the fault of his uncertain eyes, not yet accustomed to accurate vision.

EPILOGUE TO THE MERCHANT'S TALE: "For the love of God," the Host exclaims, "preserve me from a wife like that." But his own wife has faults, he admits, including a shrewish tongue; but he does not care to expound on those faults since his remarks might be reported back to her, and because his powers are unequal to the task in any case. (Here a fragment ends.)

THE SQUIRE'S TALE

INTRODUCTION: The Squire's Tale is a romantic story which evokes something of the strangeness of the East and the awesomeness of occult phenomena. It is an unfinished story, but even the part that Chaucer left shows a prolixity, and a curious interest in descriptions of color, form, and gesture that is well suited to the young squire, who has been pictured as "syngynge ... or floytynge, al the day" and "embrouded ... as it were a meede."

INTRODUCTION TO THE SQUIRE'S TALE: The host asks the Squire to tell a tale of love, but he refuses and offers to tell such tale as he can, asking to be excused if he says aught amiss.

THE SQUIRE'S TALE: (Part One)

At Sarray in Tartary lived a noble king named Cambyuskan, an excellent ruler in all respects—brave, wise, rich, merciful, and just. He had two sons, Algarsyf and Cambalo, and a daughter named Canacee. (The Squire declares that he lacks the rhetorical skill to describe her beauty adequately.) It was the twelfth year of Cambyuskan's reign, and he was presiding at a rich and solemn celebration. To describe the splendor of the setting would take a Summer's day.

Suddenly, after the third course of the meal, and in the midst of joyous minstrelsy, a knight entered the hall riding a steed of brass. In his hand he carried a mirror of glass, on his thumb a gold ring, and by his side a naked sword. The knight greeted the king and his company so graciously that Gawain could not have done better, and delivered his message in a manly and skillful fashion. He was sent by the King of India and Arabia to deliver the gifts of steed, mirror, ring, and sword. The steed (simply by the turning of a pin) could carry its rider wherever he wished to go—and within the space of twenty-four hours; the mirror had the virtue of showing the king any adversity taking place in any quarter of his realm (or of showing any fair lady the infidelity of her lover). The ring imparts the power to understand the language of the birds, and to know the medicinal virtues of herbs. The sword could cut through any armor and deliver wounds that could be healed by applying the flat of the sword to the flesh. The ring was given to Canacee, and the horse was left in the hall to be examined by all. Many admiring and curious speculations were made about the gifts, theories of magic and occult influence expounded. The courtiers chattered, judged, and described, until the king arose from the table and took his throne. The evening was spent in dancing and revelry, and continued admiration of the marvellous brass steed. When the king asked the knight to explain its operation, he laid hands upon the reins and the horse too began to trip and dance. The revels went on until daybreak.

> **COMMENT:** As in the case of the Knight's Tale, long sections of the poem are elaborate descriptions which do not admit of summary. But they reflect an interest in the rich and strange. Even the Squire is aware of his long-windedness as he (later) remarks that the "savor" of a story is spoiled by "prolixitee" and that he had better get on with it.

(PART TWO)

The revelers retired into deep slumbers, except for Canacee, who awakened after her first sleep in excitement concerning the magical ring and mirror. With her governess and other ladies Canacee walked out in the Spring morning. In the branches of a tree she spied a beautiful bird crying out in a piteous voice. It was a peregrine falcon which, swooning for lack of blood, had almost fallen from the tree. By the virtue of the ring Canacee was able to engage this gentle bird in conversation, and learned that she had been the victim of a traitorous lover—a tercelet which, having won her by his oaths and his long service, proved in the end to be a double-dealer and a "newfangled" lover.

> **COMMENT:** Like the descriptions of feast and dance, the falcon's account of the love affair (filled with the bromides of the art of "fyn lovyng") is drawn out to great length. Apparently only the fact that the bird swoons for loss of blood brings the melancholy recital to a close.

With her occult knowledge of herbs Canacee makes healing remedies for the bird, and the Squire leaves her to continue this work. He ends his second part with a promise to recite several episodes before returning to the story of Canacee: of Cambalus' intervention in the love affair of the falcon; of Cambyuskan (apparently some tales of his former wars); of Algarsyf, and how he won his wife Theodora; and of Cambalus' jousting with two brothers. Part Two ends with the line: "And ther I lefte I wol ayeyn bigynne."

(PART THREE) The Squire utters only two lines when he is interrupted by the Franklin.

THE WORDS OF THE FRANKLIN TO THE SQUIRE AND OF THE HOST TO THE FRANKLIN: The Franklin praises the Squire for his eloquence, and asserts that he wishes his own son were not the wastrel that he is, but would practice gentilesse (so apparent in the conduct of the Squire). The Host intones: "Straw for your gentilesse," and bids the Franklin keep his bargain and tell a tale.

THE FRANKLIN'S TALE

INTRODUCTION: The Franklin's Tale makes an excellent illustration of the difficulty of classifying Chaucer's tales. Every commentator feels obliged to explain that it is really not a breton lai despite the fact that the Franklin seems to identify it as such in his prologue. (The exact definition of these lais is a fairly involved matter in any case, and it seems best to note merely that the setting of the Franklin's story in Brittany and its concern with the supernatural show the influence, somewhere along the line, of the breton lai.) The tale is based upon a story by Boccaccio and it really belongs to the type of the "questioning" story. It is almost (like the Knight's Tale) a "question of love," but may perhaps be more accurately referred to as a "question of gentility." Who (of the three men—squire, knight, and philosopher) has been most open-hearted? This is the question on which the tale ends, and towards which the events lead, though the poem is concerned with other things such as the nature of "gentilesse," and is built around the folk-lore theme of the "rash promise." If there is a marriage group of tales, the Franklin's Tale is of the group; but it glances about widely at tales previously told. The love triangle (Aurelius, Dorigen, and Arveragus) falls into relationship with the triangles of the Knight's, Miller's and Merchant's tales; the themes of trouthe and gentilesse act as comments on the discussions of maistrye and "sovereignty" of the Wife's and Clerk's tales, and so forth. The supernatural has already figured importantly in a number of tales, and here it is basic to the plot structure. Considering the bizarre relationships which have characterized the marriages in previous tales, one would like to feel that the tender love of Dorigen and Arveragus is being offered by Chaucer as a kind of norm, but it is (unhappily) made to flower under most peculiar and trying circumstances. The poem is not exceptionally well suited to the Franklin as he has been envisaged in the General Prologue (among other things, he was "Epicurus owene sone"—a pleasure-loving householder), but it is brought into connection with him at the end of the Squire's tale, where he expresses the wish that his son might learn the sort of gentilesse which the Squire so happily illustrates. All in all it is one of the more appealing of the Canterbury Tales, and it provides a fitting counterpoint to the bitter irony of the Merchant's Tale.

THE FRANKLIN'S PROLOGUE:

The Franklin asks to be excused for his rude speech, and pleads that he has never studied Cicero nor learned the art of rhetoric. The only colors he knows (as opposed to the "colors" or decorative figures of rhetoric) are the colors of the meadow flowers or the paints and dyes of artisans.

THE FRANKLIN'S TALE:

There was once a knight (of Brittany) called Arveragus, who served his lady, Dorigen, long and well. For "pity" of his pains and woes she agreed to take him as her husband and her lord; he in turn swore never to assume "maistrye" over her, but to obey her as any lover ought, save that for appearance's sake he would be thought to have the "sovereignty" in his own house. Pledging her "trouthe" she promised to be a humble and true wife to him. (Here the Franklin, obviously adverting to the Wife's and Clerk's discussions of marriage, condemns "maistrye" and emphasizes the necessity of patience. Harsh words, he notes, are often uttered in anger or in grief; a man may not seek vengeance for every wrong done to him.) After a year of wedded bliss, Arveragus decided to travel to England for a year or two to seek honor in battle. In his absence Dorigen wept and sighed—mourned, wailed, and fasted. Distraught for love of Arveragus, Dorigen took such little interest in the world that her friends tried every device to comfort her, warning her that she was killing herself without cause. But just as one can by long application engrave an impression in a stone, so these friends (aided by letters from Arveragus) eventually won her back from sorrow.

Dorigen's castle stood near the sea, and though she tried for diversion to walk along the cliffs this merely increased her sorrow, both because she was reminded that none of all the incoming ships carried her beloved husband, and because the sight of the "grisly rokkes blake" made her apprehensive for her husband's safety when he should return. At times she would reflect on the terrible unreason of a world which contained such a foul "confusion of a werk."

> **COMMENT:** It has often been noted that the rocks play a central part in the tale from the standpoint of theme and character as well as plot. Dorigen's fearful reactions to the rocks anticipate her tender refusal of Aurelius, and support the ideas of "derke fantasye" and "magik natureel" so prominent in the tale; more importantly, perhaps, it is the removal of the rocks which puts Dorigen in the power of Aurelius and brings about the several manifestations of "trouthe" with which the tale is mainly concerned.

In her solitude Dorigen would question the very governance of God, in permitting their existence: "Lord, " she would say, "why have you created such an unreasonable work? It does no good to man, bird, or beast. If man is so fair a part of your creation that he has been made to your own likeness, why do you permit a hundred thousand men to be slain by rocks? I will leave all disputation to men of learning, but would to God that all these black rocks were sunken into Hell!"

Seeing that walks by the sea were of no avail in overcoming Dorigen's grief, her friends attempted to divert her with dancing, games, and the delights of a garden. Among the dancers was a young squire named Aurelius, who for two years had been in love with Dorigen, never daring to reveal his secret to her. Because he was a neighbor and a man of honor, Dorigen fell into conversation with Aurelius. When he spied an opportunity the squire revealed his great passion and asked Dorigen to have "mercy" on him. Dorigen sharply turned aside Aurelius' protestations, but added (in a playful tone): "The day you remove all the rocks along the coast of Brittany, that day will I give you my love. I offer my "trouthe" in pledge of this."

The wretched Aurelius went home in desperation, and vainly pleaded with Phoebus to bring a flood to cover the rocks so that he might be able to say to Dorigen: "Keep your promise — the rocks have disappeared." Swooning in unfulfilled desire, Aurelius fell into a trance. Meanwhile, Arveragus, now the flower of chivalry, returned and resumed his blissful life with Dorigen. Aurelius lay for two years in the pain of unrequited love before he was able to set foot on ground. His only comfort was his brother, who wept and wailed over the plight of Aurelius, and finally thought of a solution. In Orleans, when he had been a student, a fellow of his had come upon a book of natural magic which taught the art of "apparences," by which objects were made to seem to disappear. Holding forth the hope of removing the black rocks through magic the brother persuaded Aurelius to make the trip to Orleans. Even before they reached the city a clerk (using occult powers) met them and announced that he knew the reason for their visit. Aurelius quickly dismounted and went to the home of the magician, where he was treated to a marvellous display of "apparences." After supper the magician learned of Aurelius wish to remove the rocks of Brittany and agreed to carry the matter out for a thousand pounds. Returning to Brittany with his "tables of Toledo," his roots, his centers, his arguments, his equations, and all the multifarious skills and tokens of his craft, the magician soon brought it about that the rocks would seem to have vanished for a week or two.

Aurelius fell at the magician's feet in gratitude, and went off to make his triumphant announcement to Dorigen. He left her pale in astonishment and disbelief. "Never did I think it possible," she exclaimed, "it is against the orderly course of nature!" (There now follows a "complaint to Fortune," in which Dorigen cites several examples of maidens and wives who chose death rather than dishonor, among whom were the daughters of Phidon, Stymphalis, and Lucretia. Intending to take her own life, Dorigen continued her lament for a day or two until Arveragus returned from a brief journey. With tears and remorse she gasped out her grievous tale. Arveragus took the news with "glad chiere" and "in freendly wise," and told Dorigen to "hold her trouthe" for "trouthe is the hyest thyng that man may kepe."

COMMENT: It is obvious that the Franklin places a high valuation on the virtues of the social class represented by the Knight and the Squire. "Trouthe," one recalls, is the first of the characteristics of the Knight — "trouthe and honour, fredom and curteisie." Among the many limited visions of human love in previous tales which this emphasis on "trouthe" illuminates, the Wife's utter materialism may well be paramount. Speaking of infidelity, she has said: "He is to greet a nigard that wol werne/ A man to lighte his candle at his lanterne; / He shal have never the lasse light, pardee."

After mastering his feelings long enough to make this magnanimous gesture, Arveragus breaks out weeping, and commands Dorigen never to breathe a work of the misadventure they must endure. When Dorigen explained her husband's action to Aurelius, he too, not to be outdone in magnanimity by a knight, released Dorigen from her bond and plighted his "trouthe" in promising never to hold her to the agreement. After ransacking his coffers (to add to his woe) Aurelius found that he had to return to the magician with only five hundred pounds instead of the promised thousand. The magician, when he heard of the generosity of both Arveragus and Aurelius decided — not to be outdone in "gentilesse" by either knight or squire — to remit Aurelius' debt. He took his horse and went his way. "Lordynges," the Franklin asks, "which of these was the most generous, in your opinion?" (Here another fragment ends.)

THE PHYSICIAN'S TALE

INTRODUCTION: The Physician's Tale is the (very brief) story of Appius and Virginia, told by the Roman author Livy, and here taken by Chaucer from the Romance of the Rose. It resembles an edifying legend more than any other type of story, particularly in Virginia's confrontation of the unjust judge, and in her firm resolve to submit to death rather than to the lustful desires of Appius. The Physician's Tale is connected with the Pardoner's Tale, but there is no other evidence of Chaucer's intentions concerning its final position in the grouping. Not much has ever been made of its possible relationship to the themes of previous tales, though its similarity to Dorigen's lugubrious examples of "death before dishonor" has been noted. There is also a rather obvious slap at the Wife of Bath in the Physician's remark: "For al to soone may she (a young maiden) lerne loore / Of booldnesse, whan she woxen is a wyf." The tale is not especially well suited to the Doctour of Phisyk as he is presented in the General Prologue (satirically), but it is apt enough for a physician if one chooses to emphasize his professional interest in a beautifully formed human person, and to ignore the caricature of a venal doctor which has always been the stock-in-trade of satirists. The introduction, which includes a praise of Nature for her work in forming Virginia, is an attempt to make clear its suitability to the doctor.

THE PHYSICIAN'S TALE: There was once a knight named Virginius, who had a beautiful daughter (Virginia). Nature had taken great pains in forming her fair body.

> **COMMENT:** The Physician's opening is actually a long rhetorically conventional statement by the Goddess Natura, asserting her superiority to earthly artists like Pygmalion and Appelles, and establishing her position as "vicaire general" (deputy) to the Lord in His work of creation.

The Physician goes on to say that Virginia was as beautiful in soul as in body, given to humility, abstinence, patience, discretion — a paragon of womanly virtue. So modest and constant in heart was she that she would feign sickness simply to avoid scandalous company.

The Physician then addresses himself to governesses in charge of noble lords' daughters, and asks them not to feel insulted if he suggests that they hold their positions for one of two reasons: either they have managed to preserve their chastity; or, they have forsaken an earlier life devoted to the "olde daunce" (of love) and thus have an excellent knowledge of the pitfalls confronting a young maiden. "There is no guardian like a reformed thief."

> **COMMENT:** This is all connected to the main theme of tale, in view of the fact that "of alle tresons sovereyn pestilence / Is whan a wight bitrayseth innocence." This is of course the crime of Appius, the judge.

So prudent was Virginia, however, that she needed no governess. One day, on her way to the temple, she came under the eye of a high officer, a justice named Appius. Knowing that he would never be able to persuade her to sinful acts, he decided upon more subtle means. By threatening a low fellow with the loss of his head for refusing to be an accomplice, he arranged it so that the churl was to accuse Virginius of keeping the maiden as his daughter when in reality she was his own thrall, stolen from his house by night. The case came before Appius, the perjurer told his lies, and Virginia was made a ward of the court, pending her eventual return to the accuser. Virginius returned home "with fadres pitee stiking thurgh his herte," and told Virginia that there was no recourse, but that she would have to die by his own hand. Asking only for a brief space to lament her fate, she went willingly to her death, happy to die a maid. When the judge heard of this he ordered Virginius to be hanged, but the people (who had now a firm conviction of the accuser's lies, and Appius' treachery) rose up and cast him into prison, where he hanged himself. The accuser was condemned to a death by hanging also, but through the intervention of Virginius his sentence was commuted to exile. Such are the fruits of sin!

THE PARDONER'S TALE

INTRODUCTION: The <u>Pardoner's Tale</u> is justifiably one of the most popular of the Canterbury tales with modern readers. The macabre story of the three rioters who go off in search of Death so that they may slay him (and find death in a totally unexpected but ironically proper way), is an exemplum set in a sermon recited for the pilgrims by the Pardoner. He offers the sermon as a sample of his preaching methods. The ironies in the entire Pardoner episode may ultimately defy analysis, but briefly they come down to this. The Pardoner is a thoroughly depraved, self-seeking individual. He knows this — and he admits it to the pilgrims. The theme of all his sermons, as of this one, is: "Radix malorum est cupiditas." That is, "the love of money is the root of (all) evils." Through the brilliance of his rhetoric he can persuade people to turn away from the very vice which he is practicing as he condemns it. The question of the suitability of tale to teller in this case can hardly be entertained. The portrait of the Pardoner, the prologue to his tale, the tale itself, and the dramatic facing-off of Host and Pardoner following the tale, are all masterfully woven together.

WORDS OF THE HOST TO THE PHYSICIAN AND THE PARDONER: The Host cries out upon the perjured churl and the "fals justise" which the Physician has told about, and exclaims: "Allas, so pitously as she was slayn!" He then (with his typically pointed jesting) turns to the Physician and says: "Truly, my master, I pray that God will spare your noble body, and your urinals, your chamber-pots, your Ipocras, and your electuaries (all tools of the trade). I cannot use the proper terms but I swear that your grievous story has almost given me a cardiac attack." He then calls on the Pardoner for some tale of "mirthe or Iapes;" the "gentils" immediately object to the ribaldry which they are sure the Pardoner has in mind; the Pardoner agrees to tell "som moral thyng" but calls for a drink of ale to aid his memory.

PROLOGUE OF THE PARDONER'S TALE: (The Pardoner describes his preaching technique). Lordings, my theme is always the same — "the love of money is the root of all evils." First I display all my letters and seals, then I sprinkle my speech with a few Latin phrases (to stir up devotion), and then I show them my "relics:" an old sheep's bone, which I tell them wards off the pox and all other diseases from animals, and multiplies a man's store of earthly goods (it also cures jealousy); and a mitten, which multiplies whatever amount of grain a man might sow (so long as he makes a suitable offering".) "Good people," I say, "if there is any among you who has done a grievous or shameful sin, he will have no power to make an offering in this church. But I invite the virtuous among you to come up and make your offerings, and I absolve you by the power which has been granted to me." This trick has been good for a hundred marks a year. I stand up in the pulpit, my hands and my tongue going a mile a minute, and preach earnestly about avarice (though my whole purpose is only to loosen their purse-strings). Many a sermon, indeed, arises from evil intentions. I also have the knack of pinpointing accusations without actually mentioning names. Thus I spit out my venom under the guise of holiness. But as I said, my theme is always "the love of money" and even though I'm guilty of it myself I can make others repent.

COMMENT: The Pardoner's arrogant pride in vicious triumphs over weak and superstitious minds, his insulting vanity in addressing the pilgrims (at the end of his sermon-tale) as if they too were credulous fools, and his physical oddities (described in the portrait) combine to form a picture of psychological complexity which has baffled critics. The Pardoner may well be the most interesting example of Chaucer's peculiar blending of abstract and conventional details with directly perceived human characteristics.

Do you think I want to live in poverty (he asks); I like money, rich food, wine and wenches. But you wish to hear a tale. Well, I may not be a moral man, but I can tell a moral tale.

THE PARDONER'S TALE:
In Flanders there was once a group of young revellers, given to drinking, dancing, and gambling — night and day. They swore great oaths, laughed at sin, and in their gluttonous behavior, allowed the fires of lechery to be kindled in them (The Pardoner here indulges in a lengthy rhetorical declamation against gluttony, which he blames for the incestuous act of Lot, Herod's slaying of John the Baptist, and the sin of Adam and Eve. And he details the sinful pleasure of eating luxurious food, ending in the apostrophe: "O wombe! O bely! O stynkyng cod! (bag) / Fulfulled of dong and of corrupcioun!" How the cooks carry out their lecherous inclinations in wasting nothing that will pass through the gullet softly and sweetly! He then offers an equally long attack on wine and drunkenness (also a form of gluttony), and follows this with a diatribe against gambling (which leads to lies, deceit, blasphemy, waste, and loss of honor) and against false oaths.

These three rioters, he continues, early one morning heard the clinking of a funeral bell. Upon learning that it signalled the death of an old fellow tavern-haunter, they swore an oath to go out and hunt down this "false traytour Deeth," and starting up in a drunken rage set out for the village where death had last struck. On the way they encountered an extremely aged man who revealed that through God's will he was forced to wander about the world until he could find a man who would exchange youth for age.

COMMENT: The figure of the old man has provoked much interesting comment, and several attempts to explain him — ranging from "death" itself to the Wandering Jew. Despite the inability of students to give him a precise identity, the dramatic impact of the old man is obvious — he embodies their collective "sins" against the natural process of aging, and he is the instrument by which they find gold, and consequently, death.

Learning that they were in search of Death, the old man (under threats) sent them up a lane to an oak tree. Running to the tree they found almost eight bushels of gold florins; realizing, however, that they had to wait for cover of darkness to carry it off they decided to send one of their members for bread and wine, while the other two stood guard. As soon as he left, his companions, from greed, decided to stab him to death. He too, however, his mind captivated by the beauty of the florins, came to the same decision, and went to the shop of an apothecary for some rat poison. Filling two bottles with the poison, and a third (for himself) with wine, he returned to the oak. "Need I say more?" inquired the Pardoner. "Thus did these two slaughterers, and the poisoner, come to an end." (Still illustrating his sermon technique, the Pardoner once more declaims against "cursed sin," and blends homicide, gluttony, lechery, gambling, blasphemy, and false oaths into one sin of unnatural proportions.) "Now, good people," he says to the parishioners, "come up and make your offerings. I will enter your names promptly, and absolve you by virtue of my high authority." Then, turning to the pilgrims, he adds:

> . . . . . . and, lo, sirs, thus I preche.
> And Iesu Crist, that is our soules leche,
> So graunte yow his pardon to receyve;
> For that is best; I wol yow nat deceyve.

COMMENT: This is one of the most famous problems in Chaucerian criticism, even if it be assumed that there is no doubt that the remark is addressed to the pilgrims rather than the hypothetical parishioners. Is it a dropping of the mask of arrogance, and a serious pang of remorse and penitence? Or is it a piece of impudence — an attempt to convince the pilgrims that a genuine religious feeling lurks beneath the cynicism?

The Pardoner then invites the pilgrims themselves to come and make offerings to his relics and receive his pardon. The Host ought to be first, the Pardoner opines, since he is most enmeshed in sin. The Host, dropping perhaps for the first time his tone of jocularity, makes an attack on the Pardoner, with a strong hint of insult concerning his physical deficiencies. The Pardoner becomes speechless with wrath, and only the intervention of the Knight, with a command for a kiss of reconcilement, restores the mood of amity and jollity.

THE SHIPMAN'S TALE

INTRODUCTION: With the Shipman's Tale we return to the tone and setting of the fabliau, though the plot is a version of a type of folktale referred to as "the lover's gift regained." The tale was obviously first intended for a woman, probably the Wife of Bath, and many possibilities exist for bringing it into relationship with other tales (the Merchant's, for example), though there are no clear indications of any definite position in the grouping. Chaucer probably had not come to a final decision on the matter. The general air of scurrility which pervades the poem makes it appropriate enough to the rascally Shipman, though the assignment (once the idea of a woman-teller had been rejected) was by no means an inevitable one. There is a considerable amount of punning in the tale (frequently vulgar), which increases the difficulty of reading it with full understanding. The action, plot, and characterization, however, are clearly drawn, and the main meaning and the general humor of the situation are obvious.

THE SHIPMAN'S TALE: A rich merchant of St. Denis had a beautiful, companionable, and fun-loving wife. He kept a good house, and had numerous guests, among whom was a young monk, a very close friend of the merchant (since they had grown up in the same village). The monk, because he was a very prudent man, had his abbot's permission to ride out on inspection tours of the abbey's holdings, and he was a welcome visitor at the merchant's house, (welcomed by the servants as well, since he always had a gift, for even the least of them). The merchant himself spent much time in his counting-house, and on one such occasion (early in the morning) the monk, Daun John, encountered the fair wife walking in the garden. By asking leading questions under pretense of pastoral counselling, the monk learned that the wife was unhappy—that her husband, as she believed, was the worst man imaginable, chiefly for his stinginess, but for all the six things which women desire in their husbands and which he lacked. Women wish their men to be: "Hardy, and wyse, and riche, and ther-to free (generous), / And buxom to his wyf, and fresh a-bedde."

> **COMMENT:** This is a clear indication that Chaucer, at some stage of his planning, brought the tale into the "marriage group" and connected it with the question of what it is that women most desire, which is of course the main theme of the Wife of Bath's Tale.

As it turned out, the wife, in desperate need of one hundred franks, asked the monk to lend it to her, promising to repay it in pleasantries of whatever sort he might desire. Daun John promised to get the money for her, and deliver her out of her cares, at such time as her husband was away on a trip to Flanders.

The night before the merchant's departure, the monk took him aside and asked for the loan of one hundred franks, promising to repay him, whatever might betide. The merchant gladly lent him the money, and went off to Flanders where he comported himself just like a merchant (neither dancing nor gambling—all business). The next Sunday the monk returned, and (for his previous generosity to the servants) had the freedom of the house. He gave the wife the hundred franks and had his will of her, returning to the abbey with no suspicions having been raised. Upon the merchant's return he visited the monk (ostensibly to ask about his welfare). Daun John alleged that he had given the money to the merchant's wife—who knew by certain tokens what it was for. The merchant went home happily and spent the night in mirthful occupations with his wife. But in the morning he scolded her mildly for having taken payment from the monk, and thus embarrassing him when he went to collect the debt. The wife was not at all abashed, pretending to have no knowledge at all of the purpose of the hundred franks. In fact, she thought it was money to be spent on herself, and had laid out every penny of it on clothing. Seeing that there was no remedy, the merchant had to forgive his wife.

COMMENT: The force of the ending of the tale depends to a great extent on the punning use of the terms of business dealings, particularly on the ambiguity of the word "debt," which can be taken as a reference to the debitum maritale ("marital debt"), though there is also some rather vulgar double-entendre—appropriate enough to the Shipman.

WORDS OF THE HOST TO THE SHIPMAN AND PRIORESS: The Host compliments the Shipman, and then, with almost excessive politeness, asks the Prioress for a tale.

THE PRIORESS'S TALE

INTRODUCTION: The Prioress's Tale is an example of a very popular type of pious legend known as a "miracle of the virgin." They were quite commonly found in sermon handbooks, and varied in degree of subtlety and popular appeal, though they always involved the miraculous intervention of the Blessed Virgin Mary in the life of some person (usually a sinner) who had a special devotion to Our Lady. In some of the more extreme examples the most perfunctory sort of devotion, practiced by an otherwise thoroughly abandoned sinner, resulted in his salvation. In one legend a sinful monk who used to leave his monastery every night and swim across a river to keep his unholy appointments never went by the statue of the Blessed Virgin without genuflecting and repeating the words "Ave Maria," even though he was hardly aware of what he was saying. Returning one night, he tired and drowned. As his sins were being weighed in the celestial balance, the devils jumped on to add weight to his evil deeds, but the Blessed Virgin put one finger on the side of his good deeds, which sufficed to load the balance in his favor and save his soul. The legend of the Tumbler of Notre Dame (who practiced his only talent—tumbling—before Our Lady's statue, and was carried off to heaven by a flight of angels through her intercession) is perhaps the best known story of the type. It is significant that the Prioress is given an example which involves a young and innocent child, and it has often been noted how well this suits not only her status as a woman and a religious person, but also the extreme sensibility which Chaucer has attributed to her in the General Prologue. (She would, for example, weep at the sight of a mouse in a trap.)

COMMENT: In view of her unrestrained outbursts against Jews modern readers have sometimes imagined Chaucer to be satirizing what he conceived to be an anti-Semitic strain in the Prioress's piety. While this is not entirely out of the question, it should be noted that it is just as likely that Chaucer was merely registering in a non-committal way his familiarity with the deplorable attitude toward Jews common enough in medieval Christendom, and certainly given wide currency in in the "miracles of the virgin," which often presented such a view. Of course it is quite possible that the Prioress's lamentations over the martyred child vis-a-vis her easy acceptance of the awful reprisals against the Jews is a piece of Chaucerian irony.

THE PRIORESS'S PROLOGUE: The prologue is really a hymn to the Blessed Virgin, which, by extolling the gentle virtues of Mary as maid, Mother, and Queen of Heaven, makes a fitting introduction to a tale which concerns a young child, and is to be told by a nun—especially committed to the protection and guidance of Mary.

THE PRIORESS'S TALE: In a great city of Asia there was a Jewish quarter, maintained by a lord for his usurious purposes. It was open at both ends and men could walk or ride through it. At the farther end of this community there was a school for Christian children. One of the pupils was a widow's son, seven years of age, who had a great reverence for Our Lady. As he sat in school he used to hear the older boys learning to sing the . . . . . . on Alma redemptoris mater ("Gracious mother of the Redeemer"), . . . y careful attention he was able to get the entire first verse by hear . He was too young to understand the Latin but he had an older schoo.-fellow explain the meaning to him. Even though he should be beaten for not learning his primer the youth (upon learning that it was composed in honor of the Virgin) resolved to learn it all before Christmas. His fellows taught him the words and he sang it twice a day, coming and going to school, and just as he was passing through the Jewish section. In their hatred of Christianity the Jews determined to do away with the boy; they hired a murderer who, without delay, caught the boy, cut his throat, and threw his body into a privy.

> **COMMENT:** The Prioress here indulges in a rhetorical outburst against the Jews, and extols the martyrdom and virginity of the boy. She anticipates the conclusion of the tale in the proverbial statement (best known for its occurrence here in Chaucer's poem): "Mordre wol out, certeyn, it wol nat faille." That is, "Murder will out."

The poor widow waited the long night through, and in the morning searched high and low for the boy, calling upon the Mother of Christ. Finally she went to the Jewish quarter, and after searching further, found the boy in the pit. But lo! the miracle! This gem of chastity and bright ruby of martyrdom, began (though with throat cut) to sing Alma redemptoris so loudly that the place rang with the sound. The Christians gathered quickly, and after praising the King of Heaven and His Mother, had the Jews bound. The child was removed with a great procession to the abbey, while all the Jews who had any knowledge of the murder were drawn by wild horses and later hanged. The abbot inquired of the boy how he was to sing, inasmuch as his neck was apparently cut. It was through the power of Christ and because of the worship of His Mother that he had the gift, answered the boy. The Virgin had come to him before he died and, laying a grain upon his tongue, commanded him to sing O Alma. Only when the grain should be removed would he cease his singing and die. The abbot removed the grain and the boy gave up the ghost. The assembled crowd wept and praised the Mother of God; later they erected a marble tomb for the boy's body. The Prioress ends with a reference to the death of Hugh of Lincoln, alleged to have been slain a century before by Jews.

SIR THOPAS

INTRODUCTION: Sir Thopas is one of the two tales assigned to Chaucer himself as narrator. It is a delightful spoof of a type of popular, jingling romance, known as "tail-rhyme romances." Even if one were totally unfamiliar with Thomas of Erceldoune, however, or other examples of the type, he would have no difficulty recognizing the poem as a satire on exaggerated literary versions of deeds of knight-errantry. The most humorous aspect of all, of course, is that Chaucer should have given himself this dreary sort of tale to narrate.

PROLOGUE TO SIR THOPAS: The Host directs his attention to Chaucer, remarking, in effect: "What manner of man are you? You're always staring at the ground as if you expected to come across a hare. Come over here, and look a little more cheerful. Move back, my lords, and give the fellow room. His waist (Chaucer was quite short and stout) is as ample as mine. In fact, he looks like a puppet or an elf. Tell us a tale of mirth, my good fellow." "Host," answers Chaucer, "don't be ill pleased, but the only tale I know is a rhymed tale I learned long ago.'

SIR THOPAS: Of course Sir Thopas is not really a tale but a burlesque of literary clichés, and thus does not lend itself too well to summary. It begins:

> Listeth, lordes, in good entent,
> And I wol telle verrayment
>   Of mirthe and of solas;
> Al of a knyght was fair and gent
> In bataille and in tourneyment,
>   His name was sir Thopas.

> **COMMENT:** The humor is partly a result of the repetition of tags like "fair and gent," and "of mirthe and of solas," partly of the jingling rhyme, partly of the absurd name "Sir Topaz." (The topaz was a symbol of chastity.) Later stanzas continue the idea of exaggerated chastity, conventional but silly marvels, and cowardice.

Sir Thopas was born in Flanders; he was a doughty swain; his lips were red as the rose, and he had a "seemly nose;" he could hunt the deer, ride a-hawking, shoot the bow, and win the prize at wrestling. Many maidens mourn for him, "But he was chaast and no lechour." He rides over plain, and through forest, observes the flowers and hears the birds, falls in love at the sound of the song-thrush, dreams that an elf-queen will be his bride, and goes to the land of Fayerye to find her. He meets a great giant, Sir Olifaunt (i.e. Elephant), and arranges to do battle with him on the morrow "whan I have myn armoure." The giant hurls stones at him but he escapes, "and al it was thurgh goddes grace, / And thurgh his fair beringe." (Chaucer continues in the same vein with a description of the armor of Sir Thopas. Then he begins a second "Fit" but is interrupted by the Host.)

HERE

THE HOST STINTETH CHAUCER OF HIS TALE OF THOPAS: "For

the love of God, no more of this," says the Host, "my ears are fairly aching with your worthless speech. You're only wasting time; let's see if you can entertain us with something in prose." "Gladly," replies Chaucer, "I'll tell you a little thing in prose. But just as the Evangelists come to the same conclusions, even though they vary in some particulars, I will repeat some proverbs that you have heard before, though I may vary the language somewhat. But the essential point will be the same as that of the little treatise I am following.

> **COMMENT:** There is a joke here in the fact that Chaucer speaks of a "litel thing in prose," and of a "litel tretis" and a "tretis lyte," but rambles on in what must seem an endless fashion to the pilgrims.

THE TALE OF MELIBEUS

INTRODUCTION: The Tale of Melibeus is in prose. It is a rather close translation of a French original, and it has usually been regarded as a fairly dull performance. The tale is a treatise rather than a narrative, though there is a very thin line of action involving an attack on a daughter of Melibeus and his coming to a decision as to the kind of vengeance he will seek. When the tale is defended, it is usually on the ground that medieval audiences had a taste for sermonizing that is lacking in modern readers. It is suited to Chaucer as narrator only in the perverse sense that it is so far below his normal level of artistry that it is almost funny.

THE TALE OF MELIBEUS: A mighty and rich man named Melibeus was out in his fields one day when his house was attacked. His wife was beaten and his daughter was given mortal wounds in her feet, hands, ears, nose, and mouth. (The rest of the tale is a debate (which consists mainly of the quotation of proverbs) between Melibeus and Prudence, his wife, in an attempt to decide what action he should take. He wishes to take vengeance; she recommends peace and forgiveness, and finally prevails. He forgives his enemies entirely.)

THE MONK'S TALE

INTRODUCTION: The Monk's Tale is a series of short biographies concerned with the fall of famous men—what the Middle Ages described as "tragedies." This view is connected with the medieval idea of the wheel of Fortune (discussed in the Introduction to the Knight's Tale) and is described by the Monk as follows:

> Tragedie is to seyn a certeyn storie,
> As olde bokes maken us memorie,
> Of him that stood in greet prosperitee
> And is y-fallen out of heigh degree
> Into miserie, and endeth wrecchedly.

The sub-title to the tale is a pretty clear indication that Chaucer was following Boccaccio's De Casibus Virorum Illustrium (Concerning the Fates (lit. "Falls") of Illustrious Men). The melancholy contemplation of horrible examples seems to have been more suited to medieval tastes than the exaltation provided by high tragedy as we know it in the plays of Aeschylus or Shakespeare. Chaucer of course knew nothing of Greek tragedy, and these so-called "tragedies" stem from the Boethian vision of the uncertainty of the world, and have much more in common with the late medieval "dance of death" theme. There are seventeen instances treated by the Monk: five Old Testament figures; two from apocryphal Biblical story; five from classical legend and history; four from contemporary history; and one from early medieval history. The Monk speaks in his prologue of having a hundred such stories to relate, and when the Knight interrupts him after seventeen, we may take this both as Chaucer's way of ending a tale which has no clear narrative structure, and as a commentary on the sort of mind which knew no moderation in its dwelling on grievous thoughts. On the surface the tale is quite well suited to the idea of a monk as a withdrawn contemplative—not so well adapted to the figure of the "hunting monk" which we are given in the General Prologue.

THE MONK'S PROLOGUE: When Chaucer finishes his tale of Melibeus the Host remarks that he wishes his wife Goodelief might have heard it. She knows nothing of the sort of patience represented by Prudence, the wife of Melibeus. When Harry beats his servants she brings him huge clubs, and cries "kill the dogs—break their backs." When she fancies she has been insulted she accuses Harry of being a coward if he does not seek vengeance for it. His life with her is a continual battle. "But enough of this," he says, "my lord, the Monk, tell us a tale." The Host then proceeds to offer some good-natured but cutting banter on the subject of the Monk's probable prowess as a lover.

> **COMMENT:** By this time in the course of the pilgrimage the jokes about clerics who don't live up to their vows of chastity are wearing a little thin. A similar passage at the end of the Nun's Priest's Tale, which is undoubtedly genuine, occurs in only four of the manuscripts of the Canterbury Tales, and it may be a sign that Chaucer felt he had worked the vein out and was going to cancel it.

The Monk listens patiently, and then announces that he is going to recite some tragedies (see above), and asks to be held excused if he forgets to keep them in the proper chronological order.

THE MONK'S TALE: "Lat no man truste on blind prosperitee; / Be war by thise ensamples trewe and olde."

(LUCIFER) Once the brightest of angels, he is now plunged into misery from which he can never escape.

(ADAM) Created directly by God, there was never a man of such worth; yet for "misgovernaunce" he was driven out of prosperity and condemned to labor and mischance.

(SAMPSON) Sampson was noble, strong, and consecrated to God. He killed a lion with his bare hands, and slew a thousand men with the jawbone of an ass. His strength lay in his hair, however, and having told this to his mistress, Dalila, he was sold into the hands of the Philistines. He destroyed their temple by shaking two pillars, but he came to a wretched end by confiding in a woman.

(HERCULES) Hercules was a "sovereyn conquerour." He killed and got the skin of the (Nemean) lion; slew the Centaur and the Harpies, stole the golden apples, and performed many other valiant deeds. No man ever slew so many monsters. He set pillars at both ends of the world. His mistress, Dejanira, sent him a poisoned shirt, which caused the flesh to fall from the bones. Not wishing to die by poison, however, he covered himself with burning coals. Fortune overthrows a man by means which he least suspects!

(NEBUCHADNEZZAR) The "royal magestee" of Nebuchadnezzar may hardly be described. He twice conquered Jerusalem and bore off the precious vessels, enslaved the children of Israel, made magnificent golden images and tried to make the Israelites worship them (but Daniel would never assent to this). Suddenly, all his dignity vanished. He acted like a wild beast, eating hay with the oxen, and walking about in the rain; his hair became like eagle's feathers, and his nails like claws, until God finally released him. Thereafter he recognized the might of God.

(BELSHAZZAR) Belshazzar was the son of Nebuchadnezzar. He was proud and an idolater, and given to drunken revelry. Feasting one night from the precious vessels stolen from Jerusalem, he saw mysterious writing on the wall, which caused him to quake with dread. Daniel expounded its meaning. By God's command Belshazzar's kingdom was to be divided between Medes and Persians. That very night the king was slain and Darius, (a Persian), came into his reign. When Fortune wishes to forsake a man, she bears away his kingdom, his riches, and his friends.

(ZENOBIA) Zenobia, Queen of Palmyra (Third Century, A.D.), was unsurpassed in hardiness, in lineage, and in gentility. She lived the life of a man, hunting wild beasts, and sleeping in the hills. She preserved her maidenhood for many years, but was finally married to Odenathus with whom she lived in joy and mutual happiness, except for the fact that she allowed him to use the offices of a husband only for the engendering of a child. They had two sons. With her husband she conquered many lands. After his death she continued to exercise a mighty power over the land. But Fortune mixes gall with honey. Aurelian, when he came to the governing of Rome, conquered Zenobia, and enslaved her and her two sons. Allas, Fortune! She that was once looked on with awe, is the common spectacle; she who wore the crown, now wears a cap; she who bore the sceptre, now bears the distaff.

(KING PETER OF SPAIN) Noble Peter, the glory of Spain, held high in majesty by Fortune, you were betrayed and slain by your brother.

(KING PETER OF CYPRUS) O worthy Peter, who won Alexandria by "heigh maistrie," your own liege-lords slew you in your bed. Thus Fortune brings men to sorrow!

(BERNABO OF LOMBARDY) Great Bernabo, Viscount of Milan, and the scourge of Lombardy, your nephew had you killed in prison—how, I know not.

(UGOLINO OF PISA) No tongue may tell of the awful suffering of Earl Ugolino of Pisa. He was imprisoned with his three children (the oldest being scarcely five). They were to be starved to death. Pitifully wasting away, and calling out for bread, the youngest died. Ugolino began to gnaw his own arms from grief. Thinking it was from hunger the remaining sons offered their own flesh to their father. They died within a day or two. Ugolino himself, in despair, died from starvation also. Fortune carved him away from high estate!

(NERO) Although vicious, Nero held the entire world in subjection. He loved delicately embroidered and gem-encrusted garments. He even had fish-nets made of gold. From the delicacy of his imagination he burned Rome, slew senators just to hear how people wept, committed fratricide and incest, and slit his mother's womb to see the place of his engendering. He had his old master, Seneca, slain because he dared to rebuke him. The people finally rose up against him, and as he fled in disguise he quaked to hear the insults hurled at his name. He prayed to his gods and sought refuge in a garden where he found two rough fellows whom he begged to decapitate him (so that nis body would not later be defamed). He slew himself, and Fortune laughed at the sport!

(HOLOFERNES) There was never a man of fiercer strength, of higher renown, or of greater pomp than Holofernes. Fortune kissed him sweetly but led him up and down so that his head was off before he knew it. He made the whole world give up their gods and pay worship to Nebuchadnezzar. But as he lay drunk one night Judith, a woman, stole into his tent, cut off his head, and stole away again bringing the head to town with her.

(ANTIOCHUS) Who needs to repeat the venomous deeds of King Antiochus and how he fell from great prosperity and died wretchedly? Fortune had so smiled on him that he thought he could reach the stars. He hated the Jews and thought to destroy Jerusalem, but God smote him with invisible and incurable ills (a reasonable punishment, considering the bodily pain he had caused others). He did not shrink from his purpose, however, and prepared an army. But his pride and boasting were laid full low when God spilled him out of his chariot so that he had to be

carried about in a chair. Worms crept through his organs and he stunk
so badly that his followers avoided him. In his evil day he knew God
indeed for Lord of all creation. In stench and horrible pain he died
wretchedly on a mountain. Such a reward does pride receive!

(ALEXANDER) Alexander was the greatest conqueror the world has
ever seen. He was the heir of Fortune's honor. Except for wine and
women nothing could keep him from deeds of arms, so full was he of
leonine courage. He reigned twelve years and then was poisoned by
his own people. He rolled a seven but Fortune turned it into snake-eyes.
Yet she wept never a tear!

(JULIUS CAESAR) Through wisdom, manhood, and great effort, Julius
Caesar rose from humble estate to become emperor of Rome, and ruler
of the western world—until Fortune came to be his adversary. He slew
Pompey but it was not long before Brutus conspired against him and
decided upon the place where he was to be stabbed to death. One day
he went to the Capitol, and false Brutus and others ran their daggers
into him. So manly was he that even as he lay dying he threw his mantle
about him so that he would not lie exposed. Fortune was first a friend
and after a foe. No man may count upon her favors for very long.

(CROESUS) Rich Croesus, king of Lydia, was caught in the midst
of his pride and led to a spot where he was to die by fire. But the heavens
shed such a rain that the fire was quenched and he escaped. (Fortune was
saving him for a death on the gallows). He thought (wrongly) that his
escape meant that he would never be slain by enemies and he planned
new wars. He had a dream that confirmed him in this folly, but his
daughter explained it to him correctly. The tree (in the dream) is a
gallows; Jupiter means snow and rain; Phoebus is the sun. You are going
to be hanged; rains will wash you and the sun will dry you out. Fortune
always strikes with unexpected blows. As soon as men begin to believe
in her, she fails—covers her bright face with a cloud. (Here stinteth
the Knight the Monk of his Tale.)

THE NUN'S PRIEST'S TALE

INTRODUCTION: Chaucer's story of Chauntecleer the Rooster, and
his wife, Pertelote the Hen, is first of all a fable about typical "hen-
pecked" husbands, and typical fussy wives, who like to cluck "I-told-you-
so's" at their unfortunate mates. (A fable, of course, is a story in which
the main characters are animals who represent human beings—not
necessarily specific persons, but types of individuals.) Secondly, the
tale is a mock-heroic poem. (A mock-heroic poem uses the language
and the devices of a serious epic poem, but applies them to a trivial
or ridiculous subject.) Thus, the treatment of a rooster and a fox as if
they were Hector and Achilles, battling for the city of Troy, makes the

Nun's Priest's Tale the earliest mock-heroic poem in English. Sir John, the Nun's Priest, is not described in the General Prologue, but there are scattered references in the links which show him to be a pleasant man with a sense of humor, though it is strongly implied (in the fact that he rides such a nag) that he is somewhat under the thumb of the Prioress. The tale is very aptly placed after the Monk's tale. His serious and flowery set of stories on the theme of high tragedy has really overdone things, and the Monk has apparently taken it all with great earnestness. In any case the mood of a pilgrimage was often high-spirited, and ordinary rules of conduct simply did not apply. Thus a story which dealt with barnyard animals spouting philosophy and poetry had just the sort of dream-like unreality proper to the atmosphere of Springtime "high-jinks." In this respect it resembles the Squire's Tale somewhat.

THE NUN'S PRIEST'S PROLOGUE: Just as the Monk is in full stride, telling one tragic story after another, the Knight (by virtue of his social standing) interrupts him. He tells the Monk that a little gloom goes a long way, and asks him to recite a happier tale if he knows one. Let's hear about a poor man who rises to great fortune, he says.

> **COMMENT:** Though the Knight has a right to object to the boring tragedies of the Monk, his own preference for "rags-to-riches" themes may be meant to indicate a deficient taste on his part. If so, there may be some substance to the complaint of prolixity in the Knight's own tale.

At this point the Host, Harry Bailly, agrees with the Knight. He calls the Monk a loud-mouth, and asks, "What's the point in crying over spilt milk? There's no pleasure in that." He then adds that he would certainly have fallen asleep, if it hadn't been for the jingling of the Monk's bridle bells. Harry then calls on the Nun's Priest for a tale.

THE NUN'S PRIEST'S TALE: Sir John, the priest, begins in a leisurely way. He describes a dairy farm, owned by a poor widow, who lived in a very run-down house, ate the simplest of meals, and had only a few animals. Among these animals, however, was a cock, named Chauntecleer, whose crowing was the loudest (and the most accurate) for miles around. Chauntecleer was a beautiful fowl, gaily colored, and looking for all the world like burnished gold. Not the least of the reason's for Chauntecleer's pride was his fair wife, the hen Pertelote.

> **COMMENT:** The name "Chauntecleer" means "clear-singer;" both Chauntecleer and Pertelote were typical names for a hen and a rooster—they were not invented by Chaucer. His description, however, is significant. They are treated as if they are royal warrior and lady. This "humanity" and "nobility" ill fits the barnyard setting; this works not only to comment on the previous tale, but to call attention to the discrepancy between human pretense and aspiration, and the frequently sordid reality underneath it.

The priest reveals in a solemn tone that one night Chauntecleer had been disturbed by an ominous dream. He had a vision of a beast which looked like a dog, but was yellow and red, and had its ears tipped with black (a fox, of course, though Chauntecleer had never seen one, and there-fore couldn't have identified it). The cock was greatly frightened by this dream, and to add to his discomfort Pertelote accused him of cowardice. "Are you afraid of dreams," she asks, "God knows, there isn't an ounce of truth in them." She then goes on to explain that dreams are simply the result of overeating and indigestion, or else of a person's psychological makeup. A melancholy person, for example, tends to dream of black bears or black bulls.

> **COMMENT:** At this point, the story is slowed up with the business about dreams, so that Chaucer can get in a few digs at the expense of carping wives. There may have been a few such wives at court, though it is just as likely that it is directed at wives in general, represented on the pilgrimage by the Wife of Bath.

Pertelote's solution to Chauntecleer's problem is startlingly simple. Take a laxative. She then proceeds with a long catalogue of fourteenth-century laxatives, which includes some foul-smelling herbs and (of all things) worms. Chauntecleer thanks his wife for her learned advice, but insists that his dream is not due to indigestion but is, in fact, a prophecy of a terrible fate in store for him. So he gets back at her long-winded recital by telling two stories to illustrate his point. The first concerns two good friends who happened to be travelling in a strange country, and couldn't find a double room for the night. One had to sleep in a barn with the oxen. The traveller who had the good luck to get the single room was startled out of his sleep by an awful dream. In it his companion screamed for help—he was being murdered. The friend, thinking dreams to be of no importance, turned over and went back to sleep. The dream continued, and in it the murdered man revealed that after he had been slain for his gold, his body had been hidden in a dung cart. Only in the morning did the dreamer realize the essential truth of dreams. Not finding his companion in the barn, he searched for him and too late discovered that every detail of the dream was accurate.

> **COMMENT:** The story is a bit far-fetched, even for an audience that did have an open mind about dream significance. But as an argument against Pertelote's theory of indigestion Chauntecleer is quite proud of it.

At this point Chauntecleer gets so excited about the idea of murder, that he goes into a long harangue, ending in the famous statement (repeated from the Prioress's Tale): "Murder will out, this is my conclusion." Breathless as he is, the cock has still another story to relate. This one also involves two friends. They were to go overseas on the next day, but one man dreamed that certain drowning was in store for them. He refused to budge forth, but the other friend, laughing him to scorn, set sail. Mysteriously, in full view of other vessels, the ship's hull sprang a leak and went down with all hands. (Chauntecleer is so impressed with the effect these stories seem to be having on Pertelote that he can't stop himself.) He recounts the legend of Saint Kenelm, who foresaw his own murder in a dream; he reminds her of the feats of dream interpretation performed by Daniel and Joseph in the Bible; and he alludes to the Trojan hero Hector, and to his wife's dream (borne out by events) that he would be slain. "This dream of mine means bad luck," he shouts, "and you can keep your laxatives, they won't help <u>me</u>."

> **COMMENT:** Chauntecleer's references to Daniel and Hector, and other heroes, as if his case could be considered comparable to theirs is all part of the fun of the mock-heroic poem. But the very fact that he even considers Pertelote's notions about laxatives, makes his plight even more ridiculous. Chaucer is showing us here, as elsewhere in the poem, that when we are most serious in our own eyes we are frequently ridiculous in the eyes of others.

Chauntecleer now decides to behave a bit more civilly toward his wife, and proceeds to compliment her on her beautiful face. He quotes a Latin phrase ("In principio, mulier est hominis confusio") as an added compliment, telling Pertelote that it means "Woman is man's sole joy and bliss."

> **COMMENT:** The Latin is a garbled phrase, but it means something like "From the beginning, woman is man's worst enemy." The mistranslation accomplishes three things:
> 1. It adds to Chauntecleer's foolish arrogance.
> 2. It is ironic (since the dream later proves to have been a true vision) that Pertelote, by pooh-poohing Chauntecleer's dream, really <u>is</u> acting against his best interests.
> 3. We, as readers, see that there is a level of truth in the Latin statement; all the way back to Adam and Eve there <u>have</u> been women who were their men's worst enemies.

Leaving Chauntecleer in the height of his pride and arrogance, the Nun's Priest turns his attention to the fox (Daun Russel is his name, we later learn). He has been lying in a bed of weeds, waiting an opportunity to pounce on the rooster. The priest, with tongue in cheek, cries out on the fox as a traitor, worse than Judas or Ganelon (the traitor in the French epic, the <u>Song of</u> Roland). He then goes into a lengthy discussion of Divine foreknowledge. (This was a popular question in the fourteenth century—if God knows the future, doesn't that <u>determine</u> all our acts?) It really has very little to do with the story, but the idea that a fox pouncing on a rooster might be considered serious enough to be regarded as a subject of Divine foreknowledge supports the mock-heroic tone.

The priest finally gets back to the main plot, and relates that Chauntecleer, as he was watching a butterfly, at last caught sight of the fox. He cried out, and began to run, but the fox, in his oily way, soon convinced the foolish cock that he had not come to do him harm but only to listen to his beautiful voice. He had never heard such a fine voice, he declared, except for that of Chauntecleer's father. "Let me see," he says in a voice dripping with honey, "if you can imitate your father." Utterly disarmed by this flattery, the cock beat his wings, closed his eyes, and prepared to sing.

> **COMMENT:** Here Chaucer makes it quite clear that his tale refers to human beings as well as animals, and he even suggests strongly that there may be a specific application to lords and courtiers at the court to which he is attached.

Seeing his chance the fox seized Chauntecleer by the neck, and bore him off toward the wood. Like wives whose husbands had been cut down in battle, the hens set up such a clucking that the widow and her two daughters were aroused. In an instant they set up a hue and cry, and with the shouting of the people, the barking of the dogs, and the various noises of geese, ducks, and bees, there was a terrible hubbub—such a to-do that it seemed the heavens were falling. But Chauntecleer still had an ace to play. "If I were you, "he whispered to Daun Russel, "I'd turn around and scream a few insults at those churls." "You're right," the fox answered, but as he opened his mouth to shout, the cock quickly broke loose, and flew up into a tree. The fox, of course, tried to lure him down again, but it was no use. Chauntecleer had learned a hard lesson and he was not to be caught again.

COMMENT: The final comment is the priest's comment, as he emphasizes once more the lesson this fable teaches. "Any of you who imagine that this tale is only a humorous jest about a fox, a cock, and a hen, look a little deeper for the moral. Remember the words of Saint Paul: 'Everything that is written is written for our instruction.' " One of the main precepts this tale certainly illustrates is this: Pride goeth before a fall. But there is undoubtedly an important significance in the fact that the Nun's Priest illustrates it in a way so different from the Monk.

(Here a fragment ends.)

THE SECOND NUN'S TALE

INTRODUCTION: The Second Nun's Tale is Chaucer's version of the legend of Saint Cecilia. It is typical of the sometimes naive but frequently charming stories which make up the great collection by Jacobus Voragine, the Legenda Aurea (Golden Legend).

COMMENT: A legend was something like "required reading" in religious houses of the Middle Ages. (The Latin "legenda" referred to "something which ought to be read," and it was a term originally used to denote a portion of the daily office (set daily prayers). These legends in time became detached from their settings and gathered together in collections like that of Jacobus.

Naturally these stories were supposed to be edifying and they occasionally went to rather extreme lengths to demonstrate a virtue. Cecilia (who, through a mistake in translation, became the patroness of music) is here connected by Chaucer with the idea of legitimate busyness (the contrary of idleness), and the prologue develops this notion at great length. The tale is of course very appropriate to the Second Nun, even though she is not described in the General Prologue, simply by virtue of the fact that she is a nun.

SECOND NUN'S PROLOGUE: Idleness (the Second Nun maintains) is the minister and the nurse to vice, and we ought to do our best to avoid it. The Fiend is constantly on the watch, so that catching someone in idleness, he may get him into his snares. It is neither good nor profitable. Suiting action to my words, I shall here do my "feithful bisynesse" in translating the life and passion of the maid and martyr, Saint Cecilia.

(The invocation to Mary) (This is a hymn, based upon a section of Dante's Divine Comedy) Mary, flower of virgins, help me to record the death of this maiden who, through her merits, won eternal life and had the victory over the Fiend. Maid and Mother, who ennobled human nature by being the vessel in whom Eternal Love took on human form; thou, who hast magnificence, mercy, goodness, and pity; thou, who art a physician to human souls, help me, a deserted exile—give me the intelligence and the time to do my work. You who may chance to read this story which I write, forgive me for not having the subtlety to present it with great artistry.

(Interpretation of the name "Cecilia," according to Jacobus.) "Cecilia" means: (1) heaven's lily—for her chaste virginity, or for her white honesty and green conscience; (2) the way of the blind—for the example of her teaching; (3) holiness and busy-ness; (4) lack of blindness—for her great light of wisdom; (5) people's heaven—for her clarity, magnitude, and brightness.

> **COMMENT:** This is all a result of a favorite game with medieval theologians and scientists, that of "false etymologies." For example, the third meaning (above) is arrived at by assuming (wrongly) that "Cecilia" comes from Lat. caelum—"heaven," and Lia (Lat. spelling of Biblical figure Leah), symbol of the active life.

SECOND NUN'S TALE: Cecilia was a Roman maiden of noble birth. She never ceased praying to Our Lord to preserve her maidenhood. Her family arranged for her to marry Valerian (a young pagan) but even while the organs were sounding the wedding music she was beseeching God to keep her body pure. On their wedding night Cecilia warned Valerian that she had a guardian angel who would promptly slay any man who touched her. Valerian desired to see the angel, promising that he would respect her wishes if there was indeed an angel as she said, but that if there was another man he would slay them both. Cecilia sent him to seek the holy Urban (Pope Urban I) on the Via Appia, who would cleanse him of sin. Only then would the angel reveal himself. Valerian went meekly as he was bidden and Urban wept for joy at this sign of Cecilia's power. He called out upon Christ, praising His "chaast conseil," and suddenly there appeared before them the figure of an old man dressed in white, and holding in his hands a book on which there was written in gold letters the words: "One Lord, one faith, one God, and no more, one Christendom and Father of all, above all, and over all everywhere." "Do you believe this?" said the old man. "I believe it—every word," answered Valerian, at which the vision vanished. Pope Urban christened Valerian immediately.

Returning to his chamber Valerian found Cecilia accompanied by an angel bearing two crowns—one of roses, one of lilies. The angel told them to preserve these crowns with clean thoughts and chaste bodies. No one would ever see them who was not himself chaste, and a hater of villainous conduct. Valerian asked if his brother Tiburce might also be made a believer; this too the angel granted, and Tiburce found himself transformed by the sweet odor which seemed to penetrate his heart. "Is this a dream?" he asked. "Up to this time we have been living in a dream," replied Valerian, "only now do we live in truth." Tiburce agreed to be converted, and posed only some mild protestations: "Do you mean to send me to Urban, who is practically an outcast? I shall be hunted down and burned as he will be." Cecilia's explanation is that this would indeed be a fearful fate, if this life were the only life, but there is a better life in another place. "But my dear sister," Tiburce again protested, "at times you speak of one God, and at other times of three. How may this be?" Her answer; just as there are three kinds of intelligence in one man, so there are three persons in one God.

> **COMMENT:** This sort of exchange of objections and answers is typical of saints' legends, particularly of missionary saints. Saint Patrick, for example, is reputed to have answered the same objection by referring to the shamrock which is only one flower, though it has three leaves.

Many other things also she explained to Tiburce, who allowed himself to be christened, and studied to perfect his learning in the new faith. In time, however, they were found out and brought before Almachius, a prefect, who commanded each of them to fall down and adore the pagan idols, ordering his officers to "swape of his heed" if any one should refuse. Encouraged by Cecilia's exhortations Valerian and Tiburce made their refusals and died the death of martyrs. Maximus, one of the Roman officers, was so moved by their constancy that he embraced the faith and began to convert many other soldiers. Almachius had him beaten with whips of lead, until he gave up his life. All three were buried in a single place. Finally, Cecilia was brought before Almachius and put through a series of questions. "I ask you," said Almachius, "about your religion, and your faith." "You have begun your queries in a foolish manner," she replied, "expecting to receive two answers to a single question." "How is it that you answer in such a rude manner?" he continued. "How so?" Cecilia persisted, "simply out of conscience and good faith. Your power is like a bladder full of wind; with the point of a needle it is destroyed."

> **COMMENT:** The questions and Cecilia's clever answers go on at some length. This ability of the martyrs to confuse the pagan judges before whom they appear is a typical feature of these early legends. Chaucer is following the <u>Legenda Aurea</u> closely, of course; yet, while the elements of the story have the kind of piously intended exaggeration which we might expect of the Second Nun, there is no way to determine how seriously Chaucer took it all. He may well have accepted it as a piece of sober history.

Finally, after Cecilia insulted the pagan gods, and taunted Almachius for his ignorance and vanity, he ordered her to be put to death in a heated bath. When it failed to end her life, he sent a messenger to behead her with a sword. Even the legally permitted three strokes could not sever the head from the body, and she lived three more days, long enough to recommend further converts to the holy Urban, and to request that her house be consecrated as a church. To this day (the nun ends by saying) men pay worship there to Christ and His holy saint.

THE CANON'S YEOMAN'S TALE

INTRODUCTION: The Canon's Yeoman's Tale is for several reasons a baffling performance. Neither the Canon nor his Yeoman have been described in the General Prologue (or mentioned at all previously) and there is a question as to whether Chaucer had planned this sequence from the beginning or simply added it as an afterthought. It concerns a worker in alchemy, a pseudo-science popular in the Middle Ages, but involved with all sorts of nonsensical theories and mystical jargon, and the question of how familiar Chaucer was with it, and precisely what his attitude may have been is not an easy one to determine. Moreover, it has two main sections, which are not notably well connected, and this raises the critical problem of just how successful the tale is as an artistically conceived whole. That it has not until quite recently engaged the attention of critics of Chaucer is due mainly, one would suppose, to the difficulty of becoming familiar with the terminology and ideas of alchemy.

> **COMMENT:** Alchemy is (in a justly famous summation) "the history of a mistake." Alchemists, believing that metals grew in the ground—that lead, over a long period of time (on the order of a thousand years) achieved a condition of perfection, i.e. became gold—thought they could accelerate this process in the laboratory. All that was really accomplished was the production of two things: a massive number of books, mainly incomprehensible because of their confusing language; and the phenomenon of the alchemical charlatan, who began probably by improverishing himself, and ended up preying upon the credulousness and greed of others and became a public nuisance which had to be controlled by legal means.

Chaucer writes in a tradition of satire against alchemists, which began much earlier than the fourteenth century, and continued long after in such literary works as Jonson's the Alchemist and some of Donne's shorter poems, like "Love's Alchemy."

THE CANON'S YEOMAN'S PROLOGUE: When the Second Nun had finished the legend of Saint Cecilia two furiously riding horsemen appeared in the tracks of the pilgrims. One (a Canon, a member of a religious community usually attached to a cathedral) was dressed in black and seemed to be traveling light. He had a double saddle-bag hanging from the crupper of his horse. He seemed a friendly fellow and his Yeoman was the soul of courtesy. The Host was glad enough of the new company and quickly asked if the Canon knew a tale he might tell. The Yeoman immediately took over the job of answering questions, and proceeded to tell all he knew about his master. He knew many tales of "mirth and jollity," had taken on many a difficult job—he was a man of "heigh discrecioun." In fact, his knowledge exceeded that of any clerk; he could pave the whole Canterbury road in silver or gold.

> **COMMENT:** This is the point, apparently, at which the pilgrims understand that the Canon is an alchemist, and the humor of the situation resides in the fact that the talkative Yeoman may give his master's game away.

The Host asked why, if his master is such a clever man, he is clothed so wretchedly. The Yeoman replied that it is not strange at all. His master is simply too wise altogether. Many a man with an over-great intelligence has been known to misuse it. Where do they reside? They hang out on the outskirts of towns, as if they were afraid to show themselves. Why is the Yeoman's face so discolored? It is from his incessant blowing in the fire. "I am so used in the fyr to blowe, / That it hath chaunged my colour, I trowe." They work hard (the Yeoman continues), they blunder around, they gaze at the fire, they borrow money, they grope after their desired conclusion—but the science is far beyond them. It will do nothing but make beggars of them. The Canon, meanwhile, had been listening to everything, and finally berated the Yeoman for "slandering" him in the company of the pilgrims. But the Host prodded the Yeoman on, telling him to pay no heed to the Canon's threats, at which the Canon, Chaucer says, "fledde awey for verray sorwe and shame." Making the most of his master's absence the Yeoman decided to tell the whole truth about alchemy, as he understood it.

THE CANON'S YEOMAN'S TALE: (Part One)   (A monologue by the Yeoman, describing the whole work of the laboratory) I have lived for seven years with this Canon, and I have to show for it nothing but ragged clothes, a leaden complexion, and bleared eyes. And I am so far in debt I'll never get out of it. No one will ever gain by this science—he will simply empty his purse and thin out his wits. When we are in the place where we practice this "elvish" craft, we really seem quite wise, we use such lofty technical terms. (I blow the fire until my heart is faint.) Let me tell you the names of some of the things and processes we use: orpiment, burned bones, iron filings, earthen pots, luted glass, the slow fire and the quick fire, sublimation, amalgamation, calcination, quicksilver (called crude mercury), but all is vain—the labor and the money. (The Yeoman's list goes on for another eighty lines) But the Philosopher's Stone is out of our reach. We spend, we hope, we go mad with loss. It is a hard life. Whenever we put on the pot and heat the metals (it happens almost every time), "the pot to-breketh, and farewel! al is go!" The metals fly around the room, and there is great wrangling over the causes of failure. But my master comes in (he always has an encouraging word) and bids us sweep up the floor and begin again. Every one of us sounds like Solomon, but: "All is not gold that glitters."

(PART TWO) (This is the actual "tale," Part One being a kind of second prologue.) The Yeoman speaks of a certain Canon in their midst who is guilty of tricks and "infinite falsnesse," who is a fiend and a Judas.

COMMENT: The kind of particularity the Yeoman uses has caused students of Chaucer to believe that the tale was originally written to be recited before a specific audience, probably consisting of Canons. This is by no means impossible, nor is it impossible that Chaucer had some dealings with alchemists, even with the alchemist William Shuchirch. It would be difficult to prove such a connection, however, and the tale is thoroughly understandable when read simply as a general expose of a charlatan's tricks.

On one occasion this Canon visited a priest in London, one who had plenty of silver to spend, and asked for the loan of a mark, promising to return it three days hence. When he actually returned it on time, the priest was marvellously happy. The Canon, ostensibly out of gratitude, offered to teach the priest something of the art of alchemy. "Let your servant go for two or three ounces of quicksilver," he said, "and when he returns I'll show you a wonder you've never seen before." When the quicksilver arrived, the Canon had the priest dismiss his servant, so they might work in secret. At the Canon's bidding the silly priest blew the fire, poured a certain powder into the crucible, and arranged the coals. While he was thus occupied, the Canon took a coal (which had a hole in it, filled with actual silver) and secretly placed it in the crucible, as with one hand he pretended to wipe the sweat from the priest's face. Naturally the silver melted and ran out of the coal, letting the priest think that it had actually been produced out of the quicksilver. Then the Canon took a piece of chalk, shaped in the form of an ingot, took a similarly shaped ingot of silver out of his sleeve and threw it into the vessel without the foolish priest's noticing a thing; he pulled out the ingot, really believing it had been made in the pot.

Still a second time he beguiled the priest. He had a hollow stick which he filled with silver filings and plugged with wax. When he used the stick to stir the hot mixture, the wax melted and the silver ran out. The mirth and joy of the priest was inexpressible. Again, a third time, he pulled the wool over the eyes of this simple soul, and by a similar substitution "transmuted" copper into silver. The "sotted" priest was gladder than a nightingale in Spring. "For the love of God," he said, "what does the formula cost? Tell me quickly." For the friendship you showed me earlier, I can let you have it for forty pounds," said the Canon, "but it has to remain a strict secret between us." The Canon went his way, and of course the priest never saw him again. (And the formula didn't work.)

(A kind of epilogue follows, in which the Yeoman deplores the craft of alchemy.) It empties purses and causes lenders to curse the alchemists. "Withdrawe the fyr, lest it to faste brenne; / Medleth na-more with that art, I mene."

The rest is a hotch-potch of apparently meaningless or contradictory statements culled from the "mystical" alchemical authors, and the Yeoman winds up by saying:

For who-so maketh god his adversarie,
As for to werken any thing in contrarie
Of his wil, certes, never shal he thryve . . .

COMMENT: This sentiment is quite similar to that of Dante in assigning the alchemists to the lowest circle of Hell because they ape the creative power of nature. In the <u>Inferno</u>, in fact, they are in the company of forgers and counterfeiters.

ere a fragment ends.)

THE MANCIPLE'S TALE

TRODUCTION: The <u>Manciple's Tale</u> is the shortest of the complete
es, except for the Physician's. Chaucer got the story of the tell-tale
·d from Ovid, and while it is clearly an example of the "why-is-it"
·e of legend (i.e. Why are the Crow's feathers black?), it is here
.de to illustrate the virtue of discreet silence. It is hard to see how
· tale is especially well-suited to the Manciple, unless his description
· the General Prologue is meant to suggest that he is a canny and close-
·uthed individual. The prologue does not link the <u>Manciple's Tale</u> to
·y which precedes, but the reference to the town of Harbledown suggests
·t Chaucer meant it to be recited in close proximity to the <u>Canon's</u>
·oman's Tale, which was told at Boughton.

E MANCIPLE'S PROLOGUE: The Host pokes fun at the drunken
·ok, who looks as though he is about to fall off his horse, and the
·nciple picks up the refrain and offers him several insults. "Close
·ır mouth," he says, "your cursed breath will infect the lot of us.
·u're nothing but a stinking swine—you must have been drinking ape-
·e." The Host asserts that the Cook has enough to do just to stay
·ride his horse, and asks the Manciple to tell his tale.

E MANCIPLE'S TALE: When Phoebus was dwelling in the world,
· was the flower of chivalry, gentility, and worthiness. He had in his
·ıse a crow—a white bird—which he had trained in the art of speech.
· also had a wife, whom he loved more than his life, and whom he
·died earnestly to please. He was, in truth, very jealous of her. But
·t as any bird kept in a cage desires its liberty, or as a cat will leave
· silk couch to follow a mouse, so too will humans wish to be free.
·ım speaking mainly of men, rather than women, for they have a lecherous
·etite.) But, as it happened, the wife of Phoebus had a lover, a fellow
· small repute, and the white crow observed all their wanton acts.
·en Phoebus returned home, the crow told all. Phoebus, in a rage,
·w his wife with an arrow; soon after, however, he repented and berated
· bird for his false jangling. He tore out all the crow's white feathers
·l made him black, took away his power of song and his gift of speech,

and threw him out the door. (The Manciple goes on at some length
the evils of being a jangler and having a wicked tongue.) He ends
quoting his mother's words:

> My sone, be war, and be non auctour newe
> Of tydinges, whether they ben false or trewe.
> Wher-so thou come, amonges hye or lowe,
> Kepe wel thy tonge, and thenk up-on the crowe.

THE PARSON'S TALE

INTRODUCTION: The Parson's Tale is a sermon in prose on t
Seven Deadly Sins. It is from many points of view a fitting end to t
Canterbury Tales. It underlines the fundamentally spiritual object
pilgrimage; in its broad scope, touching all phases of human condu
it serves as a commentary on the limited visions of the various tal
and arguments which have gone before; and it demonstrates that the ca
of souls by the humble parish priest is the most availing and the mo
transcendent of human actions. The Parson's Tale points up his stat
as a representative of true Christian charity, and it stands out as
sharp antithesis to the many sorts of self-aggrandizement woven i
the characters of the pilgrims and the plots of the tales. The Pars
may well be the only one of the pilgrims whose tale is inevitably a
supremely right for him. (The great length of the Parson's Tale, a
the fact that it is in prose, make a summary undesirable.)

CHAUCER TAKES HIS LEAVE

In this famous "Retraction" Chaucer begs his readers to forgive h
for those things they find displeasing, and charge it to his lack of sk
And he asks that they pray for him to Christ that he might be forgi
for the "worldly vanities" which he has composed—works like
Troilus and Criseyde and the House of Fame, and many another "lecher
lay." He beseeches Christ and His blissful Mother, and all the Sai
to send him the grace of final penitence, so that he may be counted am
the saved on the Day of Judgment.

HERE IS ENDED THE BOOK OF THE TALES OF CAUNTERBUF
COMPILED BY GEFFREY CHAUCER,
OF WHOS SOULE IESU CHRIST HAVE MERCY. AMEN.

CRITICAL COMMENTARY

riticism of the <u>Canterbury Tales</u> has tended to center on individual
ales rather than on the work as a complete poem. This understandable
hen we consider the fact that it was never completed by Chaucer, and
xists only as a series of fragments, more or less complete in themselves.
he studies of Baldwin,[1] Robertson,[2] and others have emphasized the
anterbury pilgrimage as an analogue to the idea of the "pilgrimage of
an" to the Heavenly City of Jerusalem, and has thus underlined the
asically serious and spiritual nature of the pilgrim's quest and given
ae Parson the commanding position which his status as final narrator
mplies. Others have stressed the unifying framework of the <u>Tales</u>,
howing its superiority of conception to such earlier story collections as
ae <u>Seven Sages of Rome</u> and even the <u>Decameron</u> of Boccaccio or the
<u>ovelle</u> of Sercambi (which Chaucer may have known and imitated).
ollowing Kittredge's recognition of the dramatic force of the incidents
hich happen along the way, and even of the tales themselves (considered
s "speeches" by dramatic characters), Lumiansky[3] has developed at
reat length the idea of the fundamentally dramatic nature of the poem.

has also been suggested that the felt presence of Chaucer himself
s pilgrim, narrator, and observer and participator in all that goes on,
ives an underlying sense of wholeness to the work. Donaldson's[4]
ssay on the multiple nature of the pilgrim-narrator and the pervasive
ense of irony which this device makes possible, has illuminated the
aeaning of the General Prologue, and the incidents directly involving
haucer as a character. Kemp Malone's[5] observations on the Host as
ntrepreneur and general manager of the pilgrimage has also thrown
ght on the means taken by the poet to achieve an overall unity.

mong individual studies of the <u>Knight's Tale</u>, Muscatine's[6] explanation
f its rich, pageant-like, and leisurely and sweeping scope as a reflection
f the meaning of the chivalric life itself, has made a convincing defense
f a tale whose length and elaboration of detail has frequently been felt
o be excessive. Kittredge's famous explanation of the Pardoner's
stonishing reference to Christ as the only true granter of pardon (namely,
aat he has suffered a brief pang of remorse, and drops the mask for
a instant) has provoked much interesting comment, particularly on the
abject of irony in the <u>Pardoner's Tale</u>. An article by G.G. Sedgwick[7]
s an especially important example of this comment. Irony, in a more
eneral context, has been examined by C.A. Owen,[8] who emphasizes
ae subtlety and unobtrusive naturalness of the most sharply ironic symbols
a the Franklin's, Merchant's, Wife's, Pardoner's, and Nun's Priest's
les. In addition to the Knight's and Pardoner's, attention has been
rected most often to the Miller's, Clerk's, and Nun's Priest's tales.
eichner's[9] study of the characters of the <u>Miller's Tale</u> emphasizes
ae basic seriousness of Chaucer's purpose in a tale which is firmly
ooted in the tradition of popular, earthy humor. Critical analyses (like
edd's[10] of the <u>Clerk's Tale</u>) which evaluate the artistic purpose and
ae success of literary versions of folk-lore material, owe much to the
cholarly studies of Chaucer's sources—books like Severs'[11] study of the
terary genetics of the Clerk's tale of Griselda.

areful comparison of Chaucer's tales with their sources has frequently
luminated the poet's artistic purposes. Block's[12] study of the <u>Man of</u>

Law's Tale makes it clear that Chaucer must have been aware of th
general implausibility of the narrative, and added details calculate
to give a greater feeling of reality to the characters, and a more effectiv
sense of human probability to the plot. Studies of the artistic relationshi
between tales is one of the important types of criticism currently bein
emphasized. Holman's[13] analysis of the attitude toward courtly lov
in the tales of the Merchant and Franklin clarifies the function of thes
tales as mutual commentaries. The similarity of structure of the Knight'
and Miller's tales has of course often been noted, as has the unifyin
force of the "debate" on love and marriage which informs so many
the tales, notably that of the Wife of Bath.

Chaucer's advertence to contemporary life and actual people has alwa
intrigued students of medieval literature. That he may have had part:
cular individuals in mind as models for the pilgrims or for some of th
characters in the tales was the burden of an early book by Manly,[1]
and has been continued in the studies of scholars like Hotson,[15] who fin
an historical situation allegorically presented in the Nun's Priest'
Tale. His use of contemporary types rather than individuals offers a wi
field for investigation, represented, for example, by Eileen Power's[1]
study of the Prioress, and Beichner's[17] analysis of the Monk. Almo
any field of medieval cultural interest will provide information helpf
in estimating Chaucer's meaning and artistic aims. Curry's[18] study
astrology is convincing proof that the Wife of Bath's horoscope is relate
to the poet's ironic vision of the Wife. Studies of the practice of Scri]
tural interpretation show that Chaucer may have expected his audien
to be familiar with such material (Kaske's remarks on the Summoner[19]

In addition to the old standby's (Kittredge, Lowes, Lounsbury, Root, a
Tatlock), several recent book-length studies of Chaucer's poetry, fro
quite divergent points of view, deserve to be mentioned. Speirs[20] us
a modern critical approach, with an emphasis on the utility of an anthro]
ological interest in medieval life. Muscatine[21] explains the intrica(
of relationships in the poem from a stylistic standpoint. Robertson[2]
insists upon Chaucer's dependence on his audience's wide familiari
with "spiritual" interpretation of Biblical texts.

Among the less specialized, more popular treatments of the Canterbu
Tales may be mentioned the books by Raymond Preston[23] and Nevi
Coghill[24]. One thing seems certain—critical interest in Chaucer
poetry does not seem destined for an early death.

(Articles and books will be listed only by author and title—most of t
articles will be found in the critical anthologies listed in the Bibliograph
books are also listed separately in the Bibliography.)

1. Baldwin, The Unity of the Canterbury Tales (anthologized in pa
2. Robertson, Preface to Chaucer (and numerous articles)
3. Lumiansky, Of Sondry Folk
4. Donaldson, "Chaucer the Pilgrim"
5. Malone, Chapters on Chaucer (anthologized in part)
6. Muscatine, "Form, Texture, and Meaning in Chaucer's Knight's Tal
7. Sedgwick, "The Progress of Chaucer's Pardoner"
8. Owen, "The Crucial Passages in Five of the Canterbury Tale;
9. Beichner, "Characterization in the Miller's Tale"

0. Sledd, "The Clerk's Tale: The Monsters and the Critics"
1. Severs, The Literary Relationships of Chaucer's Clerk's Tale
2. Block, "Originality, Controlling Purpose and Craftsmanship in Chaucer's Man of Law's Tale"
3. Holman, "Courtly Love in the Merchant's and Franklin's Tales"
4. Manly, Some New Light on Chaucer
5. Hotson, "Colfox vs. Chauntecleer"
6. Power, Medieval People
7. Beichner, "Daun Piers, Monk and Business Administrator"
8. Curry, Chaucer and the Medieval Sciences
9. Kaske, "Patristic Exegesis; The Defense," in Critical Approaches to Medieval Literature
0. Speirs, Chaucer the Maker
1. Muscatine, Chaucer and the French Tradition
2. Robertson, Preface to Chaucer
3. Preston, Chaucer
4. Coghill, The Poet Chaucer

REVIEW QUESTIONS & ANSWERS:
DISCUSSION OF KEY POINTS

1. QUESTION To what extent does Chaucer make use of imagery in the <u>Canterbury</u> <u>Tales</u>?

ANSWER Imagery, in the sense in which that term is currently used does not figure prominently in Chaucer's style at all. That is to say he rarely uses metaphor or employs patterns of sound, color, and so forth to produce sense impressions. He does, however, make use of the ideas conventionally associated with natural objects. Animals, stones, and plants, for instance, had been reduced by contemporary speculation to a system of "correspondences"—a schematic classification according to the "virtues" they were thought to possess—and these were tabulated in Bestiaries, Lapidaries, and Herbals, respectively. Thus, the lily (<u>Second</u> <u>Nun's</u> <u>Tale</u>) was a symbol of virginity, the topaz (<u>Sir</u> <u>Thopas</u>) a symbol of chastity, and the sparrow (portrait of the Summoner) a symbol of lechery. Chaucer's "imagery" is a more intellectual device than the imagery, let us say, of Keats or Wordsworth. It is the <u>idea</u> behind the <u>thing</u> which is of paramount importance.

2. QUESTION Does Chaucer show any interest in the important philosophical and scientific questions of his day?

ANSWER Just as the theme of <u>Troilus</u> <u>and</u> <u>Criseyde</u> grows out of the tradition of philosophical questioning of the world order, verbalized for the Middle Ages in the <u>Consolation</u> <u>of</u> <u>Philosophy</u> of Boethius, so too some of the Canterbury tales address themselves to important questions The <u>Knight's</u> <u>Tale</u> is in many ways a shorter version of <u>Troilus</u> <u>and</u> <u>Criseyde</u>, showing the valiant hero and lover ultimately having to reconcile himself to "necessity" in a world of disappointed expectations. The Wife of Bath's prologue is a serious (if ironic) treatment of the important question of the rights of a married woman. The <u>Nun's</u> <u>Priest's</u> <u>Tale</u> deals (humorously to be sure) with the widely debated matter of Divine foreknowledge and human free will. And the <u>Canon's</u> <u>Yeoman's</u> <u>Tale</u> is an ironic statement of a serious attitude towards human attempts to transmute matter and "get rich quick." Chaucer is <u>interested</u> in these things but rarely is drawn into explicit statements of belief, or programs of action or reform. As an ironist he adopts an essentially non-committal point of view.

3. QUESTION Inasmuch as a good number of the tales deal with immoral, obscene, or vulgar behavior, how is one justified in calling the <u>Canterbury</u> <u>Tales</u> a great work of art?

ANSWER The question of art and morality is never an easy one to solve. A good deal of the (to us) excessive frankness, earthy humor and blunt language would have been accepted as a matter of course by fourteenth-century audiences. As for the immoral behavior of some of the characters, it should be obvious that Chaucer does not condone it If anything, the ironic conclusions of the Miller's, Merchant's, and Friar's tales, for example, expose the limited views of the characters concerned. Like most of the great comic writers—Swift, Rabelais Moliére, for instance—Chaucer saw life as a very broad spectrum of behavior. The wholeness of view, the unwillingness to present partial perspectives, is itself one of the great artistic merits of the work. It should be added, too, that there are positive correctives to the satirized actions, in such tales as those of the Franklin, Clerk, Second Nun, and Man of Law.

QUESTION Does the <u>Canterbury Tales</u> adequately reflect the richness and variety of medieval literary <u>genres</u> (types)?

ANSWER The poem has been rightly referred to as a fourteenth-century "five-foot shelf." Not only did Chaucer take pains to include many kinds of tales, but he seems to have been quite scrupulous in assigning tales to tellers on the basis of social class as well as individual personality. There are sermons, <u>fabliaux</u>, romances, legends, a "miracle of the virgin," an Arthurian romance, contemporary anecdotes, a beast fable, even a collection of "tragedies." The Knight and the Squire both recite romances, the Prioress and the Second Nun both recount pious legends, and the Miller and the Shipman both tell fabliaux. The variety in the kinds of tales is a reflection both of the rich literary tradition behind Chaucer and of the social diversity seen in the General Prologue.

QUESTION In what sense is the <u>Canterbury Tales</u> an original work of literary art?

ANSWER As in the case of Shakespeare and so many other English poets and dramatists Chaucer was not at all concerned with the invention of stories. His originality is a matter of shaping the plot, redefining the theme, and accomodating the material of his source to the particular point of view he is taking. Studies have shown that the <u>Knight's Tale</u> reshapes a story of Boccaccio so as to emphasize the theme of the nobility of the chivalric life, that the artistic reworking of the story behind the <u>Clerk's Tale</u> tends toward greater plausibility and character realism, that the <u>Prioress's Tale</u> adds material calculated to increase the sense of pathos, and so forth. Chaucer handles his sources with great freedom, adding material from a wide background of reading in the literature of his day. It is perhaps unnecessary to point out that our modern concept of plagiarism did not exist in the Middle Ages. It is in what a poet did with his sources that his real originality lay. In a larger sense, it is the total conception behind the <u>Canterbury Tales</u> that gives evidence of Chaucer's originality, the notion of uniting such a heterogeneous social group around the idea of a pilgrimage, and letting their stories reveal the meaning of the human pilgrimage through life, in a way which utterly transcends such obvious schemes as the Seven Deadly Sins, or the Vices and Virtues.

QUESTION How successful is the "framing" device used in the <u>Canterbury Tales</u>?

ANSWER Two characters are of utmost importance in the frame of the poem—the Host, Harry Bailly, and the more-or-less naive recorder of facts, Geoffrey Chaucer the narrator. The narrator is presented as a somewhat obtuse individual, lacking real powers of discrimination. His equanimity and readiness to accept as worthy of recording all things truly impressive, without making finely drawn moral distinctions, is perfectly suited to the wide range of characters he is thrown in with. Harry Bailly, as an innkeeper, may be imagined to have developed a ready way of dealing with people from all walks of life, and he amply demonstrates this talent. He is respectful to the Knight, kow-tows to the Prioress, insults many of the lower orders (especially the Pardoner), but above all keeps the stories moving. Harry Bailly, as the instigator and participant in the dramatic episodes which take place between tales, is a truly magnificent invention. The idea of the <u>Canterbury Tales</u> as an

essentially dramatic poem can be overstressed, but there is no doubt tha
much of its power stems from the dramatic immediacy of the speeche
and actions which make up the frame.

7. **QUESTION** How unique and important is the Canterbury Tales a
a document in the history of the social upheaval of the Fourteenth Century?
ANSWER The Canterbury Tales, especially the gallery of portraits i
the General Prologue, is frequently appealed to as evidence of the cor
ruption and discontent among the various orders of society, especially th
lower clergy. Chaucer's Monk, Friar, Summoner, and Pardoner, fo
example, are accurate portrayals of really existing types of ecclesiastica
officers, some of whom, no doubt, were utterly depraved. But Chaucer'
cry is not that of the moralist or the theologian. In some respects a mor
satisfactory picture of these corrupt types can be gotten from Langland'
Piers Ploughman, or from the contemporary sermon-literature (studied i
great detail by G. P. Owst, Literature and Pulpit in Medieval England)
Chaucer's voice is that of the urbane, sophisticated observer—concerned
but not crusading for reform. In his attitude toward social distinctions h
is somewhat conservative, in fact. He sees the value in a Ploughman or
country Parson, but they do not cancel out the values to be discerned in
Franklin or an elegant Prioress.

8. **QUESTION** To what extent does the Canterbury Tales reflect a
interest in the particular society of which Chaucer was a member, or i
the behavior of individuals whom Chaucer knew personally?
ANSWER It seems quite certain that some of the earlier poetry, th
Book of the Duchess certainly, and probably the Parliament of Foules an
the House of Fame, treat contemporary events at court in an allegorica
fashion. Various identifications have been proposed for the bird-lovers i
the Parliament, and while the matter has not been definitely decided, it i
generally agreed that particular human individuals are being alluded to
(The poem is of course much more than a topical allegory, and may b
read with entire satisfaction on a more universal level.) On the face of i
the bulk of the Canterbury Tales seems to have an exclusively litera
significance, though it has, for example, been suggested that the Nun'
Priest's Tale refers to real events which took place in the decade 1390
1400, that the choice of Trumpington as the locale of the Reeve's Tal
may have something to do with Sir Roger de Trumpington, and that th
Canon's Yeoman's Tale may have been composed by Chaucer in resentmen
at his having been fleeced by some contemporary alchemist. The questio
is by no means an easy one to settle; there is no good reason to doub
that Chaucer may have planted allusions to contemporary figures in hi
poems, but each possible instance must be examined on its own merits
In any case, the value of the Tales as literature will in most instances b
very slightly enhanced by the discovery of topical allusions in the text.

9. **QUESTION** To what degree is the Canterbury Tales the product o
a realistic appraisal of contemporary life—to what degree the result o
a more academic acquaintance with human society, gained from wid
reading?
ANSWER This is one of the most significant questions which can b
asked of the Canterbury Tales. We know that Chaucer was a man of th
world, experienced in war, political life, and business—that he was n
withdrawn and ascetic pedant. On the other hand he had a truly impressiv
background in literary and scientific books, and some acquaintance wit

e famous encyclopedic works of the Middle Ages, such as those of incent de Beauvais. It is the poet's unique manner of appealing from terature to life and from life to literature that gives the Canterbury ales some of its peculiar zest. It could well be said that there is a rikingly successful fusion of the social and the bookish interests of e poet in the Canterbury Tales. It is notoriously difficult to define ony, but it can at least be observed that the irony of the Wife of Bath's rologue, or of the Nun's Priest's Tale stems directly from the confront- ion of theory by practice, of books by the experiences of life.

SUGGESTIONS FOR FURTHER READING AND RESEARCH

GENERAL REFERENCE:

R. D. French, A Chaucer Handbook (1947)

TEXTS OF THE CANTERBURY TALES:

F. N. Robinson, The Works of Geoffrey Chaucer (2nd ed., 1957)
E. T. Donaldson, Chaucer's Poetry (1958)
A. C. Baugh, Chaucer's Major Poetry (1963)

TRANSLATIONS:

N. Coghill, Geoffrey Chaucer: The Canterbury Tales (1952)

CHAUCER'S LIFE:

D. S. Brewer, Chaucer (2nd ed., 1960)
Marchette Chute, Geoffrey Chaucer of England (1946)

ANTHOLOGIES OF ARTICLES ON CHAUCER:

Wagenknecht, Chaucer: Modern Essays in Criticism
Owen, Discussions of the Canterbury Tales
Schoeck & Taylor, Chaucer Criticism I: The Canterbury Tales

USEFUL READING IN LITERATURE EARLIER THAN (OR ROUGHL CONTEMPORARY WITH) CHAUCER:

Boethius, The Consolation of Philosophy
Ovid, The Metamorphoses
Dante, The Divine Comedy
De Lorris & De Meun, The Romance of the Rose
Langland, Piers Ploughman
(Anon.), Sir Gawain and the Green Knight
Malory, Morte D'Arthur
Boccaccio, The Decameron

STUDIES OF MEDIEVAL LIFE AND CULTURE:

J. Huizinga, The Waning of the Middle Ages (1924)
Eileen Power, Medieval People (2nd ed., 1954)
G. A. Plimpton, The Education of Chaucer (1935)
J. J. Jusserand, English Wayfaring Life in the Middle Ages (1930)
W. C. Curry, Chaucer and the Medieval Sciences (1926)
C. S. Baldwin, Medieval Rhetoric and Poetic (1928)
C. Dawson, The Making of Europe (2nd. ed., 1956)
E. Rickert, Chaucer's World (1948)

BOOKS ON CHAUCER:

M. Bowden, A Commentary on the General Prologue to the Canterbury Tales (1948)
G. K. Chesterton, Chaucer (1948)
J. S. P. Tatlock, The Mind and Art of Chaucer (1950)
G. L. Kittredge, Chaucer and His Poetry (1915)
Nevill Coghill, The Poet Chaucer (1949)
W. W. Lawrence, Chaucer and the Canterbury Tales (1950)
J. L. Lowes, Geoffrey Chaucer and the Development of his Genius (1934)
Kemp Malone, Chapters on Chaucer (1951)
J. Speirs, Chaucer the Maker (1951)

The advanced student might find it worthwhile to consult the following: ryan and Dempster, Sources and Analogues to the Canterbury Tales; . D. Griffith, A Chaucer Bibliography; Muscatine, Chaucer and the rench Tradition; H. S. Bennett, Chaucer and the Fifteenth Century; . G. Coulton, Chaucer and His England; J. M. Manly, Some New Light a Chaucer; D. W. Robertson, Preface to Chaucer: Studies in Medieval erspectives; C. S. Lewis, The Allegory of Love)

UBJECTS FOR RESEARCH AND CRITICAL ANALYSIS:

comparison of any one of the Canterbury tales with its source.
comparison of any one of the Canterbury tales with an analogue.
he question of the appropriateness of any tale to its teller.
summary and analysis of the recent criticism of a single tale.
haucer's use of imagery in one of the tales.
n analysis of the irony of situation in some tale.
n analysis of the attitude toward women in the Canterbury Tales.
n analysis of Chaucer's artistic use of digressions.
he relationship of some tale to the themes and questions raised by
    previous tales.
haucer's invention of dramatic incident.
ne Road from London to Canterbury.
ne medieval pseudo-sciences: Astrology, Alchemy, & Natural Magic.
    (i.e. Chaucer's use of these)
riars and medieval preaching in Chaucer.
ne Manor in the fourteenth century.
edieval medicine.
edieval Chivalry.
ourtly Love.
haucer and the great Italian authors.
edieval Rhetoric.
itire in the fourteenth century.

NOTES

NOTES

NOTES

NOTES

NOTES

NOTES

NOTES

NOTES

NOTES

NOTES

NOTES